Successful Rifle Shooting

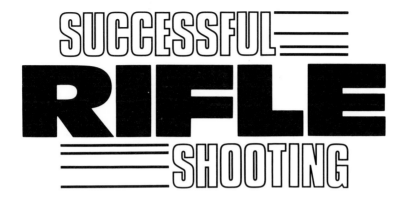

SUCCESSFUL RIFLE SHOOTING

With Small-Bore and Air Rifle

David Parish

The Crowood Press

First published in 1989 by
The Crowood Press
Ramsbury, Marlborough,
Wiltshire SN8 2HE

British Library Cataloguing in Publication Data

Parish, David
    Successful rifle shooting: with small-bore and air rifle
    1. Target rifle shooting – Amateurs' manuals
    I. Title
    799.3'12

    ISBN 1 – 85223 – 230 – 7

Typeset by Action Typesetting Limited, Gloucester
Printed in Great Britain by Butler & Tanner Ltd, Frome

Contents

Acknowledgements

The author would like to thank the following people and organisations for permission to use their photographs.

Neal O'Gorman for the photographs on pages 45 (bottom left), 46, 48 (top), 50, 54 (top), 55, 62, 63, 64, 65, 66, 67 (top), 69 (bottom, left and right), 70, 71, 74 (top right), 77 (bottom), 79, 80, 81, 84 (bottom) and 85.

I. S. Gibb for the photographs on pages 20, 39, 40, 48 (bottom), 53, 56, 69 (top), 82, 87, 88 and 89.

J. G. Anschütz GmbH for the photographs on pages 22 (top), 23 (top), 24, 25, 26, 27 (top), 28 (top), 32, 92, 93 and 94.

Mayer and Grammelspacher Dianawerk GmbH & Co. KG for the photographs on pages 22 (centre), 23 (centre) and 27 (centre).

Westinger and Altenburger GmbH & Co. KG for the photographs on pages 22 (bottom), 23 (bottom), 27 (bottom) and 28 (bottom).

Ernst K. Speith GmbH for the photographs on pages 34, 35 (bottom) and 36.

Foreword

David Parish first came to my attention thirty-two years ago when he succeeded me as British Champion Small-Bore Rifleman. In those days prone rifle shooting held sway and only a few were involved in the 'grunting and groaning' disciplines of standing and kneeling. David was one of the first to blaze the trail in British shooting which culminated in the 1988 Olympic success when Malcolm Cooper retained the Gold Medal.

David was the Rifle Coach in Seoul and his selection recognised his vast experience as a rifleman and coach at the highest level and his encyclopaedic knowledge of the shooting sports.

But this book fills a gap in the shooting library. There are books for beginners and some fairly esoteric books for the very good international shooter looking to win medals at major events. This book offers advice, guidance, direction even, on techniques, attitudes, and equipment which, if followed, will convert the tyro into the expert and, subsequently, the master shot.

It is essential reading for anyone with the will and determination to begin the climb to the higher levels of achievement.

Group Captain Dennis King, MBE
Secretary,
National Small-Bore Rifle Association

Introduction

Shooting is arguably the world's largest competitive sport – age and strength are not barriers and participants may be under ten or over ninety. There can be few sports where so many people can compete and for such a large part of their life – one shooter over eighty years of age won an Olympic medal although that was now many years ago. Once the 'bug' has bitten it so often becomes a lifetime sport or preoccupation.

There are many different disciplines in rifle, pistol, shotgun and crossbow shooting, but this book is intended to cover the target shooting disciplines in small-bore rifle and air rifle. Some countries have adopted one or other discipline as their national or most popular form of shooting. In West Germany it is the 10m air rifle; in the Netherlands 15m kneeling with the small-bore rifle; in Switzerland the 300m rifle, where every village has a good 300m range. In the majority of English-speaking countries the prone position with the small-bore rifle has the greatest following, but this has been noticeably changing over the last thirty years. It is interesting to note that the majority of trophies presented in the early part of the twentieth century and before were not given for prone shooting alone, so it is not only the influence of international shooting but also a reversion to former practices, with shooting in other positions becoming increasingly popular.

The world governing body is the Union Internationale de Tir (UIT), founded on 7 July 1907, to which over one hundred countries belong. Each continent has its own body, Europe's, for example, is the European Shooting Confederation, and although the international rules are formulated by the UIT, most countries have adopted similar rules for their own events. However, it comes as no surprise to learn that English-speaking countries' rules generally differ more than other nations' from those of the UIT; for UIT-style events they are the same, but for national competitions it is not only the distances that may be different, in yards as well as metres, but also the continuation of the longer ranges for small-bore of 100 yards or metres. Often the courses of fire, rules governing equipment and position and when sighting shots may be used differ. However, equipment conforming to the UIT rules may be used in national competitions without disadvantage, whereas equipment designed for use in national competitions may not be legal for the UIT.

Most clubs will have rifles and other equipment for the new entrant to the sport to use until such time as he or she wishes to purchase his or her own. Whilst we are mentioning 'he or she' it should be realised that rifle shooting is the one sport in which women can not only equal men but beat them as well. Remember the dream score of 592 out of a maximum 600 shot in the 50m 3 × 20 small-bore Standard Rifle event in Titograd at the 1981 European Championships by the left-handed East German shooter Marlies Helbig. That event comprises 20 shots in each of prone, standing and kneeling and such a score is a fantastic achievement! It was not equalled until the World Cup in Munich in 1988 when Anna Maloukhina of the USSR achieved the same score. A near-perfect score of 399 out of 400 was shot in the 10m air rifle event in the 1987 Suhl World Cup by the Bulgarian shooter Vesela Letcheva. The ten ring was then only 1mm, the event is shot standing and the one shot was only

1/10mm from that ten ring; the same score was also shot by Eva Joo, a young Hungarian junior, at the European Championships at Stavanger in 1988.

In most international competitions and, since 1984, in the Olympic Games, women have separate events; however, in many national competitions men and women compete together on equal terms. Whereas in the UIT events, women have to shoot smallbore with the 5.5kg Standard Rifle this may not be the case in many countries where the national rules may allow the same rifle as the men.

This book goes into each position in some detail, because, although position is not everything as you will find out as you progress, it is necessary to have a good foundation upon which to build. It will guide the beginner along the correct path with good techniques and also assist the more advanced shooter to continue to improve. Do join the local rifle club as you will gain much more from the sport by doing so and in some countries it is necessary to be a member of a club before you may be granted permission to own a rifle, or even an air rifle. Although in many counties this may not be necessary it is still a very good idea to join a club particularly if you wish to enter competitions and improve rapidly as many clubs have qualified instructors and coaches.

1 Safety

Safety is Number One and if anyone is asked what is the most important aspect of shooting the answer must always be **safety**. Shooting, fortunately, has the reputation of being one of the safest sports, owing to the observance at all times of the safety rules and one consequence of this is that it enjoys a very low insurance premium for clubs and individuals. It is essential that this record continues for all enjoying this wonderful sport, that safety standards are maintained and a rigid adherence to safety rules is enforced. Firearms and air guns must never be loaded except when on the firing point and then only after all is clear in front of the firing point and then only when engaged in actual shooting. If a range officer is in charge of the range he or she must be in control and obeyed. Do not pick up or load the rifle until the range officer commands that this may be done, or under a specific rule if in force, that a rifle, unloaded, may be picked up. Not only should safety encompass the obvious – that when a bullet is started on its way only something in its way will stop it – but also, and equally important, the aspects of health and safety.

Hearing Protection

All guns make a noise, some more than others, but even the small-bore rifle can impair hearing if some sort of protection is not worn in the form of ear-muffs and/or correctly fitting ear-plugs. Every range therefore must provide adequate hearing protection for shooters and others in the vicinity of the firing point who may not yet have their own, and suitable warning notices must be displayed for the unknowing. The UIT has a rule – *2.8 Ear Protection*: 'All shooters and other persons in the immediate vicinity of the firing line are urged to wear ear-plugs, ear-muffs or similar protection.'

Eye Protection

The next UIT rule – *2.9 Eye Protection* – says: 'All shooters are urged to wear shatter-proof shooting glasses or similar eye protection while shooting.' This is equally sensible and many shooters wear glasses to correct vision or as a coloured filter. They also protect the eye from any particles that may try to enter, act as a barrier to the wind and make shooting generally more comfortable. Even a slight wind directly from in front blowing through the small rearsight aperture on to an unprotected eye can be a nuisance and with a strong wind it can be uncomfortable or worse.

Ventilation

When using an indoor range ensure that there is adequate ventilation pulling air from the firing point towards the stopbutt. Take advice on how this should be arranged in order not to create a nuisance by annoying neighbours with the vented air. Different places have different laws and regulations for just this type of thing so check up on them first. Good ventilation makes an indoor range more comfortable, cleaner and a nicer place to take your friends and family. Whilst talking about cleanliness, do keep the range clean and tidy. Although many ranges are first class in this respect some leave a lot to be desired.

2 The Small-Bore and Air Rifle Sport

RECREATIONAL OR DEDICATED?

Shooters tend to fall into two groups, the recreational and the dedicated, although there is much blurring at the edges. Most shooters in the western world start as recreational shooters and then get the urge to try for their club, county or national team. Many do not aspire beyond a certain stage and these recreational shooters probably get more enjoyment from their sport than the true dedicated shooter who may seek international honours. At the end of an international career the dedicated shooter will often revert to a recreational shooter or may seek to continue in the sport in another area such as coaching or administration.

One cannot exist without the other, but the dedicated shooter sometimes runs the risk of being asked to shoot in many events for which the training programme leaves little if any time. This is understandable as the local club or team naturally wants the best shooters possible, but often the dedicated shooter should and must decline, as performance or continued improvement can be slowed by shooting too often or by having a programme interrupted. It is sometimes difficult for clubs or associations to see the problem and that their time can be very limited, and sadly quite unwarranted friction can occur. The dedicated shooter's path is not always an easy one but please do try and understand that he or she has different requirements.

The junior shooter should be encouraged as much as possible for without the juniors our sport will have little future. The older shooters can find much satisfaction in helping the younger members to improve even if it means less time in which to shoot for themselves. Parents in particular should not pressure their son or daughter; parents can be the greatest help to their children but in a few instances can also, through misguided enthusiasm or wishing too much for their youngster to do well, hinder their progress.

RIFLE RANGES

Rifle ranges differ considerably between those constructed for the UIT events and those outdoor ranges constructed primarily for prone events. The UIT-style ranges require certain minimum requirements for the comfort of the shooter and for protection from the elements and particularly to avoid the wind on the body. Many of these ranges are most elaborate and of fine construction and may well have their own restaurants and club rooms built in. This is how ranges should be; in direct contrast to these are the prone ranges which in some countries may or may not have a surfaced firing point and usually only a simple overhead cover for protection from the rain or sun. Some do not even have a firing point cover so that when it rains the shooter and all the equipment gets wet. These ranges also tend to be more open than the UIT-style ranges which have overhead baffles for safety and walls enclosing the range which makes for different, but not necessarily any easier, wind conditions from those experienced on the more open ranges.

The indoor ranges also vary considerably,

A modern 50 and 300 metre firing point. Tables are used for the prone; kneeling and standing with the front part folded back.

some are first class but others unfortunately leave much to be desired not only in location but in facilities, and cleanliness, the last for which there is no excuse. Some are admittedly very old, but improvements could be made for the benefit of all. Indoor ranges for small-bore rifle are usually at 25yds or 50ft, although in the former case proportionate targets are also available for 15 and 20yds if the longer distance cannot be accommodated. A few are at 15m and some even at 50m.

COMPETITIONS

The small-bore and air rifle competitions can be divided into those shot under UIT rules and those shot under national rules. The UIT disciplines are shot world-wide with little variation, apart from range peculiarities or type of target equipment. The UIT divide events into men's and women's, whereas many nations run similar events as an open class with a separate award list for women.

UIT Events

The UIT events for small-bore rifle are shot at 50m and for air rifle at 10m, and all time limits allowed include the sighting shots which may be taken only at the beginning of the competition or before each position, and no more sighters are permitted once the first match shot has been fired. The exception to this is if the shooter is interrupted for more than five minutes through no fault of his own, when additional unlimited sighting shots may be taken at one sighting target.

The men's small-bore events, both shot with the Free Rifle are:
1. *60 shots prone* in 1 hour 45 minutes. The old Olympic match but now called the English match.
2. *120 shots in three positions (3 × 40):* 40

shots prone in 1 hour 15 minutes; 40 shots standing in 1 hour 45 minutes; 40 shots kneeling in 1 hour 30 minutes, with 15 minutes changeover time between each position.

The women's events, both shot with the standard Rifle are:
1. *60 shots prone* in 1 hour 45 minutes.
2. *60 shots in three positions*: 20 shots prone, 20 shots standing, 20 shots kneeling, in 2 hours 30 minutes. There is no changeover time between positions and the shooter takes whatever time she may wish for each position and changes to the next position when ready, providing the overall time limit is not exceeded.

The events for the air rifle are shot in the standing position only, with the men's and women's events both shot with the same rifle; the difference being that the men shoot 60 shots in 2 hours whilst the women shoot 40 shots in 1 hour 30 minutes.

In both small-bore and air rifle events it is customary for all important competitions to be shot with one shot per target. This is, of course, mandatory for competitions shot under the auspices of the UIT or one of the continental federations and is to avoid the problem of two shots going through one hole and to be able to determine clearly the value of a shot which is not always easy with a group of shots which may cut away the scoring ring.

FINAL COMPETITIONS IN THE OLYMPIC SHOOTING DISCIPLINE

Since 1986 those events which are shot in the Olympic Games have had a final in the World Championships, Continental Championships and World Cup matches, and in the Olympic Games itself for the first time in Seoul, Korea in 1988. These events for small-bore rifle at 50m are the 60 shots prone event for men, the 3 × 40 three positional event for men and the 3 × 20 three positional event for women. At 10m for air rifle there is the 60 shot men's and 40 shot women's event.

The finals were evolved in an attempt to make the shooting sport more spectacular for the media, and certainly in the first Olympic Games in which they were held many more television cameras from the various broadcasting networks were in evidence. Although relatively few of the participants in the sport will ever reach such heights as to be able to take part in these finals, in such championships it is still important that the shooters know how they are conducted to be able to tell their friends who watch the shooting events on television. They are increasingly being adopted as part of the competition in national events so that not only are international contenders given an opportunity to train for these finals but also, because they are becoming part of the competitions themselves, shooters who may never aspire to international honours will find themselves taking part.

The results are put up after each shot before the shooters fire the next shot and when this is done quickly it can create more interest, especially if closed circuit television is used and an electronic scoreboard indicates the score for all to see. The actual scoring of targets can be done either at the butts or at the firing point depending on the type of target equipment installed.

From the traditional competition or 'Qualification Round' the top eight shooters are assigned a firing point in their order of ranking with the first placed to the left and the eighth placed to the right. The finals for the three positional events are conducted in the standing position whilst for those events which are shot in one position only naturally the finals are conducted in that position. The preparation time is five minutes, after which five minutes are given for unlimited sighting shots on one target at 50m or two targets in the 10m events. A warning is given thirty seconds before the end of the sighting period after which there is a one minute pause.

The final consists of ten shots and is conducted single shot-for-shot with the following commands for each shot:
LOAD: after this command the shooter loads his firearm or air rifle.
ATTENTION: 5 – 4 – 3 – 2 – 1 – START: the shooter then has 75 seconds for his shot in each event except the 60 shot prone match in which the time limit is only 45 seconds.
STOP: this command is given after the last shooter has fired or at the end of the firing period of 75 or 45 seconds depending on which event is being shot.

Each shot is then scored and when the score has been displayed the same procedure is followed for each subsequent shot until all ten have been fired. If there is a tie the decision is based on the highest score in the finals series, if still a tie the shooters who are tied will continue to shoot single shot-for-shot until the tie is broken.

What does not appear to be clear to those who have not been involved in the finals or who have not previously known of the procedure is the scoring of the targets. The normal targets are used but the rings are subdivided into ten so that it is possible to have a nine just making the line as a 9.0, a slightly better nine as 9.1, and so on until a very good nine not quite making the ten will be 9.9. The scoring is similar with the other rings. Until the new targets were adopted on 1 January 1989 it was possible to have an 11.0 and 11.1 for those shots very near the centre and central at 50m. Only an 11.0 was the highest at 10m. This was owing to the particular size of the the 1958 50m and the 10m targets then in use. However, with the new targets adopted in 1989 it is no longer possible to have a score higher than 10.9.

The scoring at the bigger matches is conducted on target-reading machines which electronically score the targets. However, as these machines are expensive it is possible to obtain manual scoring gauges. Naturally

The scoreboard before the start of a 60 shots prone final. As the shots are fired the scores and places will change, with the leaders on the left.

with the target-reading machines an additional enhancement is possible in that they can be connected directly to the computer and/or electronic score-board which saves time. It is the intention that the final is conducted as fast as possible but it is important for the shooter with the small-bore rifle to ensure that his rifle does not cool down between shots either by leaving an empty case or plug in the chamber.

A different technique may be required for shooting in the finals as it is a slower form of shooting with a definite pause between each shot and a fixed time limit in which to release the shot. Although the time limits are ample it is possible to get the mind on the clock instead of the job of releasing the shot. It also does mean that it may not be possible to wait out a wind condition until your chosen condition or conditions return. This will mean either adjusting the sights or more likely aiming off if the conditions warrant it. Some shooters find that they enjoy the challenge of the finals and do well whilst other equally good shooters have not yet mastered what is a relatively new addition to the traditional programme.

Non-UIT Events

Individual countries also have their own traditional events which differ from those shot under UIT rules. The great shooting nation of West Germany has as its national small-bore rifle the Standard Rifle which is shot in three positions by the men as well as the women. They also shoot at 100m in the standing position without the use of a palm rest; in the past this was shot on the UIT 100m target but in recent years it has been shot on the 50m pistol target. However, it can be said that the English-speaking nations have the widest divergence from strict UIT events, many of these being shot in the prone position only.

One of the best-known events is the 'Dewar Course', which has varied over the years. It was named after Lord Dewar who

presented the trophy which is still shot for as a postal international amongst a number of countries. Originally shot at 25yds with not everybody choosing to shoot in the prone position, it has in recent years been shot prone with each shooter firing 20 shots at 50yds and 20 shots at 100yds. With the increasing popularity of the 50m range a so-called 'modified Dewar' is shot substituting 50m for the 50yd stage. Often a double course of 40 shots at each range is shot.

Variations of 50m and 100yds are shot with a lessening amount of 50yds and very little 100m. Forty or 60 shots at 50m or 100yds is very popular with the smaller meeting often combining the two ranges for an English match of 60 shots at 50m and a 40-shots match at 100yds. The British small-bore Grand Aggregate at its national meeting consists of 40 shots at 50m, 40 shots at 100yds on the first day, the same courses of fire on the second day but reversed in order, the third day is an English match of 60 shots at 50m, followed on the final day, often in quite difficult wind conditions, by a match consisting of 60 shots at 100yds.

The British Championship in the prone position is shot in three stages, the first two of which are a modified Dewar at 50m and 100yds, with the top twenty competitors shooting 40 shots at each of 50m and 100yds. If there is subsequently a tie, which does frequently happen, this is shot off on one card of 20 shots at 100yds.

The American National Championship is a four day 6400 point aggregate, divided into two, with half being shot with metallic sights and half with the telescope. The course of fire each day is 40 shots at 50yds, 40 shots at 50m, a Dewar course and 40 shots at 100yds. Whereas the British targets are proportioned to, or the same size as the UIT targets, the American targets still retain the old ring sizes which make them very much easier. Although maximum scores are much more frequent, in fact commonplace, it is even more necessary to have a very high 'X count', as the inner ten is called. On the American target, which became obsolete in Great Britain in 1958, the 100yds ten ring is 2in in diameter but it must be remembered that the X ring is only 1in in diameter which is smaller than the British 100yd targets ten ring, so very close grouping is still required.

The competitions in both the British and American Championships and many other local competitions utilise the three card system which has multiple aiming marks on one target card. This is one of the biggest variations from the form of shooting in most countries and is not much seen outside of English-speaking countries. The shooter hangs the target himself and in most competitions it is permitted to return to the sighter at any time, even after the match shots have been started. The normal time for shooting

which consists of 20 shots plus unlimited sighting shots taken within the time, is twenty minutes. Sometimes these targets are used in three positional matches but this is less popular with the shooters than the target boxes which exhibit one aiming mark at one time. The three card system creates additional difficulties in the standing and kneeling positions as the aiming marks are at different heights. Certainly this system is cheaper than that used in Europe and elsewhere where target boxes or transporters are commonly used; however, the shooter does generally have to walk down and change the targets himself.

The air rifle events do not vary so much in the national and local competitions with the exception that they may be shot at multiple aiming marks and in some countries at shorter distances such as 6yds. With the

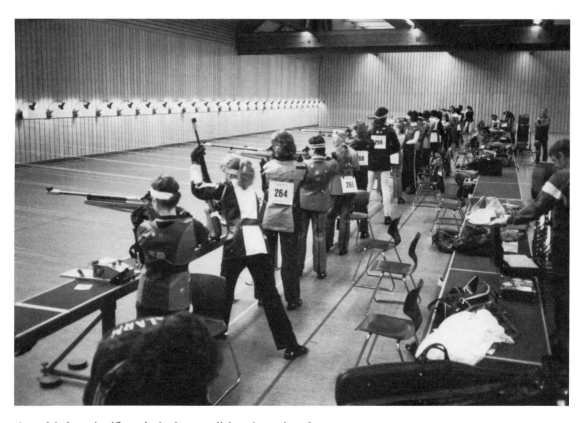

A good indoor air rifle and pistol range, light, airy and modern.

advent of the modern air rifle and CO_2 rifle, loading has become much easier and competitions for other than the standing position are now seen. For many years rifles have been fitted with a rail in the forend for sling attachment so that they may be used for training and there have been a few competitions, but now there is an increasing number of competitions for air rifle in all three positions.

Air rifle ranges can be set up in many temporary locations such as large halls and gymnasia, but it should be ensured that there is sufficient heating as many of these places can be quite cold in the winter, certainly too cold for shooting reasonably well. It is possible if sufficient space is available to set up a range in the home, but take care

An air rifle range in a gymnasium. Standing are some DDR shooters.

that no member of the family can walk across the line of shooting as although a pellet is small it can still be dangerous.

The Queen Alexandra

The Queen Alexandra is an interesting competition being somewhat different from the normal small-bore event shot in Great Britain. The trophy was first presented by Queen Alexandra, wife of Edward VII. It was originally a competition for the top shooter from each county in Great Britain and shot in deliberate, time limit, 'skirmisher' and moving target. The moving target has fallen out of favour, but the other courses of fire remain. The time limit is shot on the normal target, 10 shots in ninety seconds, single loading. The 'skirmisher' is shot on a target having 8 oval aiming marks and as many shots as possible are fired in one minute. Both the time limit and 'skirmisher' are commenced with a cartridge in the fingers but not loaded.

Nowadays there is a county team as well as an individual champion and the score on the deliberate and the time limit are both out of 200, being 20 shots with one point added for each hit on the 'skirmisher' target. It often surprises people how well they can shoot when shooting quickly (this is discussed further, later in the book) and this competition provides some very good scores on the time limit cards and totals in excess of fifteen on the 'skirmisher' even amongst those who are not so expert. It was thought that the Martini action was better for the faster shooting but it has been seen that the bolt action is the equal, if not better.

THE SMALL-BORE RIFLE

The small-bore rifle is designed to fire the .22 long rifle cartridge and can be divided into three categories – the Free Rifle, the Standard Rifle and the prone rifle.

THE FREE RIFLE

This is the rifle used by men in the three positional competitions and also by the vast majority in the men's prone events. It is also the most popular rifle in the specialist prone competitions shot in many countries. It must not exceed 8kg in weight including buttplate and palm rest if used. The word 'free' means that the rules governing this rifle are freer than those governing the other rifle but certainly not free. The buttplate has clear-cut limitations and the full details of these rules can be found in the 'Special Technical Rules for Rifle' available from the UIT.

A typical Free Rifle will have a thumbhole stock, an almost vertical pistol grip, a fully adjustable hook buttplate, and an adjustable cheekpiece. It may also have various weights and for the standing position a palm rest may be used. In addition a set trigger is permitted but on small-bore rifles these are now less popular than in past years as the current two-stage triggers are very reliable and faster in lock time than the set trigger, which is their chief disadvantage.

As this rifle is the most popular amongst those who shoot mostly prone, many manufacturers sell the rifle without the palm rest which may then be purchased separately by three-positional shooters. It is not intended to go into the pros and cons of various makes but there are currently around ten different makes of Free Rifle, and a choice can be made by trying out some of the makes and by seeing what the leading shooters are consistently using.

THE STANDARD RIFLE

This is the only rifle which can be used by women in the three-positional and the prone event under UIT rules. Until 1965 women could also shoot the Free Rifle. The Standard Rifle is also popular with many men who prefer its simpler stock design and lower weight. The maximum weight limit is 5.5kg and there are many more restrictions on this rifle. The rifle must be of conventional appearance and the buttplate may be adjustable only up or down a

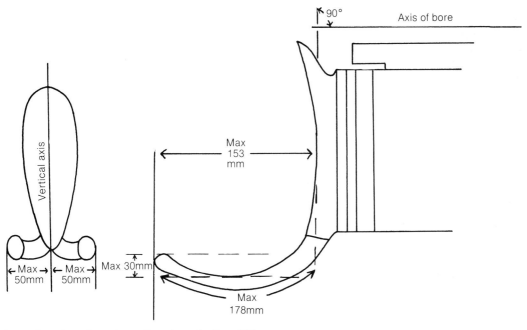

Maximum buttplate dimensions allowed on the Free Rifle.

The Anschütz Free Rifle Model 1913 with adjustable hook buttplate and palm rest.

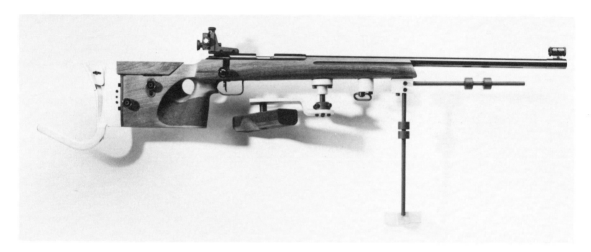

Diana Mod. 820 F Free Rifle fitted with a double stabiliser.

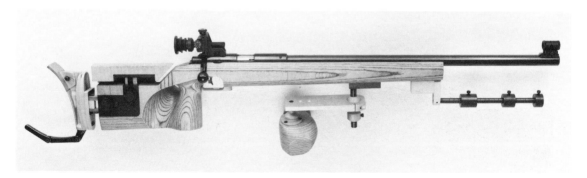

The Feinwerkbau Free Rifle with adjustable hook buttplate, palm rest and weight bar.

The Anschütz Standard Rifle, Model 1907.

Diana Mod. 820 L Standard Rifle, here fitted with a hook buttplate as an accessory which can be used in the Free Rifle but not Standard Rifle competitions.

The Feinwerkbau Standard Rifle, Model 2600.

maximum of 30mm from the neutral position. Thumb hole, thumb rest, palm rest, heel rest and spirit level are all prohibited. A removable cheekpiece is allowed but not an adjustable cheekpiece. This means that a rifle which needs a screwdriver or similar device to alter the cheekpiece is permitted but not one that can be as easily adjusted as on a Free Rifle. The stock usually has spacers to enable the length to be changed to suit the individual but, if used in the women's UIT events, once the length has been adjusted it cannot be moved during the course of fire. Exterior weights are prohibited as is a bipod or rifle rest, and the handstop or sling swivel must be removed from the rifle during the standing position. Set triggers are not permitted.

A typical rifle has a close, almost vertical pistol grip cut well down behind but not with a thumb hole. The buttplate is flat or only

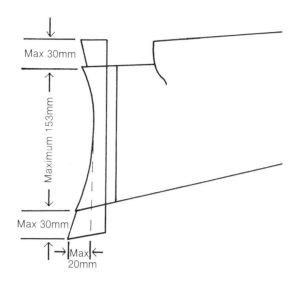

Maximum buttplate dimensions allowed on the Standard Rifle.

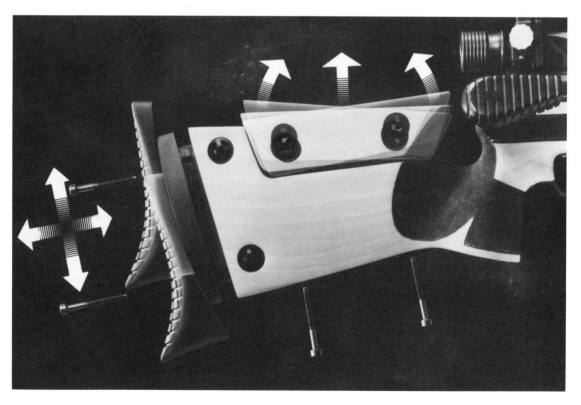

Even with the air rifle and Standard Rifle several adjustments are available to suit the individual in the buttplate and cheekpiece.

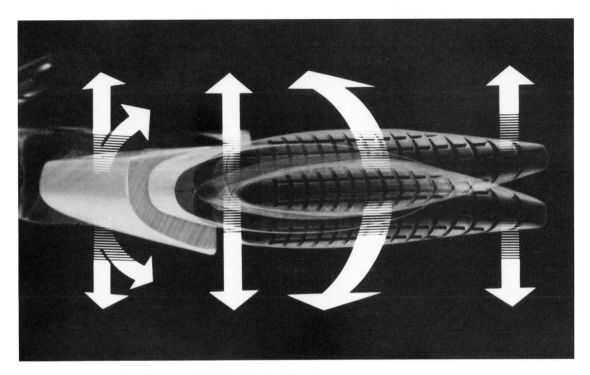

More adjustments to the side are available in the air rifle and Standard Rifle, but even if the buttplate will adjust in many directions it is permitted to offset to the left or right only parallel to the butt's centre line.

slightly curved to a maximum of 20mm. The forend is tapered so that it is much deeper in front of the trigger guard for the standing position. The stock is governed by specific rules or restrictions so that there is no doubt as to the maximum dimensions of the stock. If the factory rifle is below these dimensions the stock may be built up to the measurements permitted, providing it conforms to the existing form. Therefore if the cheekpiece is too low and any 'adjustments' are insufficient, material may be added to raise or thicken the cheekpiece. There is no restriction on the height of the cheekpiece but there is a restriction on the height of the centre of the front sight tunnel of 40mm, so if you want to be able to see through the sights the cheekpiece can be built up only so far. The length and diameter of the frontsight tunnel are restricted to 50mm and 25mm respectively.

If this rifle is used in the men's event or in non UIT events the rifle then comes within the overall rules of that event, for example Free Rifle, and may have fittings added accordingly, but then to all intents and purposes it ceases to be a Standard Rifle. About the same number of makes of the Standard Rifle are available as of the Free Rifle and the same comments apply, so see what suits and which are popular.

THE PRONE RIFLE

When used in UIT events the prone rifle either has to conform to Free Rifle rules for the men's events or Standard Rifle rules for the women's events. It is now seen infrequently in the prone events and even in such predominantly prone-specialist countries as Great Britain and the USA is not as popular as formerly. It really has few advantages for the prone position, possibly the only one being that it has no thumb hole and that it is therefore possible to shoot more quickly with the prone rifle than the Free Rifle. However, it should be possible to adjust the Free Rifle to be a more comfortable rifle for the prone position.

A typical prone rifle has a wider and flatter forend than the Standard Rifle with no increase in depth toward the trigger guard. The pistol grip and cheekpiece are shaped for maximum results in the prone position without the need for any compromise toward the other positions. The buttplate is flat or almost so and is adjustable vertically. The stock is much straighter than the other rifles with very little if any drop at the heel of the stock. As it is no longer so popular very few manufacturers make a prone rifle; although there are a number of smaller custom manufacturers to add to the few major manufacturers who still cater for this market.

The Standard Rifle is the ideal club rifle but a club should also have a few rifles of lighter weight for the younger shooter, who may find that even a rifle of 5kg or so is still too heavy. These lighter rifles are available in a number of models, usually with a lighter action and barrel and a simpler design of stock but accurate, just the same. It is important that club rifles are kept up to date

and in good order to encourage the newcomer and those who have not yet obtained or cannot afford their own rifle.

THE AIR RIFLE

The air rifle may be divided into three patterns – the spring-operated, the precompressed and the CO_2. The rifles have been developed over the years so that they are virtually vibration-free when the propellant is released. They are thus termed 'recoilless' as distinct from those with simpler mechanisms which often move considerably when shot. All must be in 4.5mm (.177) calibre.

The spring-operated pattern which for many years was very popular and won most of the competitions, utilised various methods to achieve minimum vibration, the most successful being the style which allowed the barrel and mechanism to recoil freely backward when the piston and spring moved forward. Another excellent but less popular style had an opposed piston system.

The precompressed system, whereby the shooter cocks the rifle by means of a long lever and at the same time compresses the

The Anschütz Prone Rifle, Model 1911.

The Anschütz air rifle Superair 2001.

Diana Model 100 air rifle.

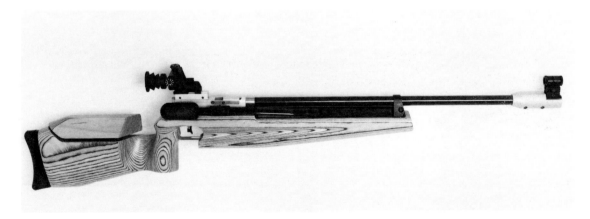

The Feinwerkbau air rifle, Model 601.

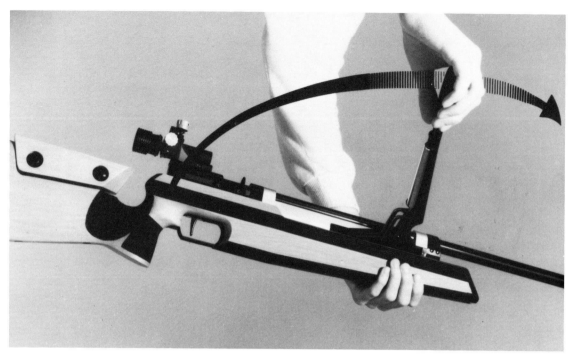

Cocking the air rifle. With modern air rifles, even the precompressed types, this is quite easy.

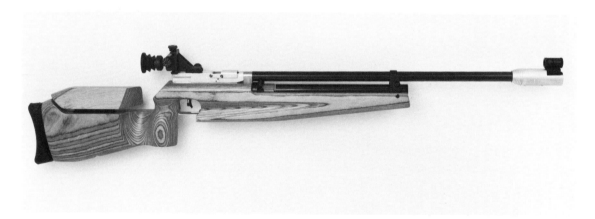

The Feinwerkbau CO_2 rifle, Model C60.

air in a chamber to be released by a valve when the trigger is pulled, has largely taken the place of the spring pattern. The problem with the early pattern of precompressed air rifle was the effort needed to compress the air, but this problem has been designed out of the current models, and the effort required has been reduced. One improvement was to alter the direction of the lever so that the shooter's arm had a better mechanical advantage. Another advantage of the precompressed system was that it was considerably quicker than the spring-operated system.

The CO_2 rifle has been around for many years both in sporting and target form but it was not until the latter part of the 1980s that really successful commercial models were produced. They are very simple to operate once the cylinder has been fitted, requiring virtually no effort. They are particularly suitable to training or air rifle competitions in all positions; the prone position with a lever-operated air rifle is difficult, especially if the loading port is far forward.

As the air rifle is mainly designed for the standing position the stock shape may be designed to give best advantage in the standing position, but it is still governed by the rules that cover the small-bore standard rifle. The cheekpiece may also be shaped to be ideal for standing without the need to compromise as may the length of the stock.

The club air rifles should consist of some full-size models together with some of the lighter junior pattern for the smaller or younger members of the club. Many of the earlier models now replaced by the latest styles are still fully competitive and excellent value but do keep them in good order.

3 Cartridges and Targets

THE .22 CARTRIDGE

The cartridge used almost invariably in the small-bore rifle is the .22 long rifle and in fact the UIT and some national associations specify no other. This cartridge of 5.6mm (.22) calibre was developed in 1887 by a New Englander named Joshua Stevens in collaboration with a ballistic engineer named W.M. Thomas. At that time, the .22 long cartridge was loaded with a thirty grain bullet and five grains of black powder. The new cartridge differed in that it was loaded with a forty grain bullet which has remained the same to this day, with a few exceptions, notably the Russian cartridge with forty-two grains and new developments of forty-five grains plus.

Other developments have included the powder being changed from black, through such as Lesmok to smokeless. An even more important development was the introduction of non corrosive priming such as Remington Kleanbore which was first marketed in 1926.

The .22 long rifle is a rimfire cartridge – that is, the priming compound is contained in the rim of the cartridge and because it has to be spread evenly around the rim to ensure ignition, there tends to be more priming compound than the ballistic engineers would prefer.

Two or three major breakthroughs when accuracy has been increased quite markedly have occurred in recent times, for example the adoption of a lower velocity of 1085ft per second (331m per second), notably by Winchester/Western in the early 1950s, and when considerable developmental work was undertaken by the British with Eley Tenex being brought out again in a new form in 1964. Other manufacturers have also developed first class ammunition such as RWS R.50 and in the early 1980s Russian Olymp, which has not been readily available outside Russia but is an outstanding product nonetheless.

The next major development in cartridges will probably be an increased bullet weight and a new shape. Perhaps an even lower velocity is possible if accuracy can be maintained. With the lower velocity, wind has less effect as the drag time is less; in other words the bullet loses less of its velocity over the distance. A faster bullet loses more of its velocity and is therefore more affected by the wind.

Headspace, the distance from the end of

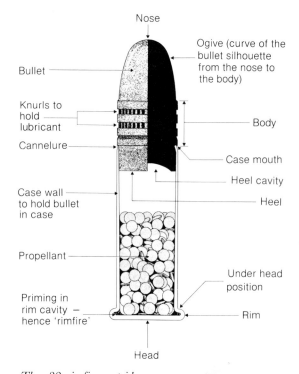

The .22 rimfire cartridge.

the barrel against which the rim rests to the bolt or breech face, is less critical than it was and some countries stipulate 1.1mm as the requirement, although for a target rifle a shade less than this may be found to give better accuracy. However, this is not something for the inexperienced to tackle and a qualified person should attend to either excess headspace or any attempt to reduce it. Certainly some shooters tend to want a headspace that is too tight and it is a matter of diminishing returns. If a rifle has adjustable headspace it can be seen that although a few batches of ammunition may shoot better groups with a tighter headspace than normal the majority may not. Headspace must never be so tight that it is less than the thickness of the rim of the cartridge as there is then the danger that the priming will be disturbed or even worse that the rim will be pinched and the cartridge will fire.

The small-bore cartridge is very susceptible to variations in ignition and it is important to have a correctly shaped firing pin striking in the correct place on the rim and with consistent force. Most cartridge manufacturers have charts showing the correct firing pin shape and the position it must strike. Always keep the end of the barrel, breech and bolt faces clean and ensure that the firing pin can travel free of any dirt or gunge which may slow its travel, to give it the best possible designed performance.

An interesting development from Krico is an electronic ignition in which the firing pin touches the cartridge case and an electric charge is placed into the base of the case, thus firing the cartridge. This method is very quick but some ammunition is not so positive in ignition.

It is noted with the small-bore cartridge that no matter how well one batch may shoot in any one particular rifle it does not follow that the same batch will shoot as well in another rifle even of the same make. For top accuracy it is necessary to batch-test your rifle, not just with a particular make but with individual batches to see what suits it,

as differences can be quite marked. This is best done from the prone position with a telescope sight and perhaps a slight rest to dampen any movement. This can be at the back of the wrist but lightly rested. Shooting with the rifle in a rest does only give an indication of accuracy of the rifle/ammunition combination and a final selection of batches of ammunition for competition use should be made from the prone position. Shoot at least four 10 shot groups and preferably more to ensure that you have the best, and this should be done both at 50m and 100yds as one batch may shoot better at one range than the other.

Nearly all rifles are now free floating with the barrel free of the woodwork without any bedding or devices touching or tensioning it. Before testing your rifle ensure that the wood is actually clear from the end of the forend to the receiver. However, it is natural for shooters to experiment and some may find that individual rifles shoot better groups with some bedding for the first 25 to 50mm of the barrel.

The way a rifle is loaded is very important; the cartridge must be placed as far into the barrel as possible each time and the bolt or action closed carefully. It is possible to enlarge the groups by some 50 per cent by closing the bolt roughly, even though the cartridge has been pushed as far into the chamber as possible before the bolt is closed. The lead in the rifling will prevent the cartridge being pushed all the way into the chamber and if the bolt is slammed shut the bullet can still be damaged and the priming in the rim disturbed. Tests have been conducted in front of disbelieving shooters to show how the group enlarges so do not waste any ammunition trying it for yourself and be a confirmed gentle closer of the bolt.

THE AIR RIFLE PELLET

Since the 1950s the air rifle and its pellet have become amazingly accurate. The pellet

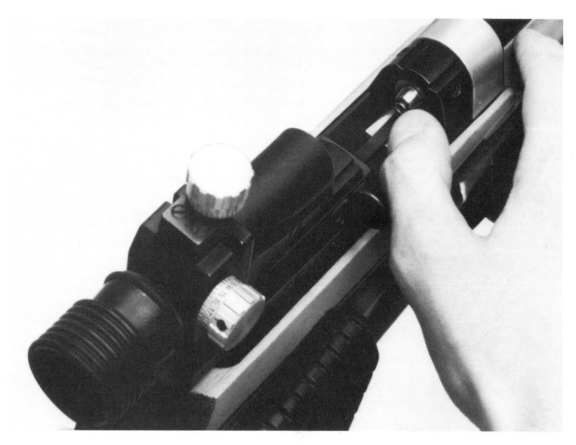

Loading the air rifle. Remember to push the pellet in exactly the same each time.

has developed until the evolution of the present style of a diabolo flat-nosed pellet, the skirt of which fits the grooves and obturates. The weight of the pellet varies with different makes and more than one weight is often made by a manufacturer to suit a particular make of rifle and whether it is compressed air or CO_2. Two manufacturers hold most of the world records between them – Heandler & Natermann (H&N) and RWS.

Pellets are made in varying sizes and it is therefore possible to obtain the size that best suits your particular rifle and barrel. Even with the very fine accuracy available it is still possible to improve upon it by matching the pellet to the barrel and, as pellets are relatively cheap compared to small-bore or big-bore ammunition, there is no reason not to do this.

Just as it is important to place the small-bore cartridge right into the chamber and push it all the way in, it is even more important to place the air rifle pellet into the barrel exactly the same distance each time; not all the way in one time and not so far the next. It is not self-contained like the small-bore cartridge and the propellant will expend its energy differently if the pellet is not seated exactly the same each time.

TARGETS

Until 1 January 1958 the small-bore 50m target had a ten ring of 20mm diameter, after which a new target was adopted to give the same scores as those obtained at 300m. This new target had a ten ring of 12.4mm diameter with a 1mm dot as an inner ten or

X ring. This target lasted until 1 January 1989 when a new target with a ten ring of 10.4mm was adopted. This size was used so that the target-reading machines used in the finals would only read up to 10.9 and not to 11.0 etc., which was confusing to shooters and spectators alike. The calculation was twice the ring width less the bullet diameter. In this case each ring was 8mm wide, hence $8 \times 2 - 5.6 = 10.4$mm.

It was felt by some that with the 1958 target scores were getting too high. Ties were becoming common and if the shooter, particularly in the prone position, was unfortunate enough to have a wild shot – a flier – owing to ammunition, it would not be the shooter's fault but could perhaps mean that he would have little chance of achieving first place or even a medal. The new smaller target is therefore more difficult but whether it will prove to be small enough only time will tell. With a small target that

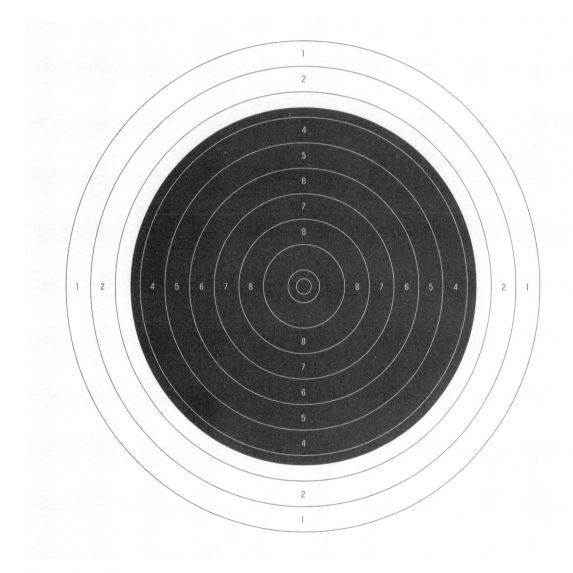

50m small-bore rifle target.

flier may score an eight but even so with lower scores the shooter may still be able to pull back.

The alternative to reducing scores internationally was the abolition of the sling in the prone and kneeling positions. This was favoured by some, but would have been rather unpopular particularly amongst recreational shooters as many national federations would probably have followed suit to prevent domestic shooting being at variance with that followed by most countries. New lighter rifles would have to be bought and possibly courses of fire changed. Imagine shooting an 8kg Free Rifle without a sling and trying to dope the wind on a difficult day!

The targets used by many countries for other distances have been proportioned to the 50m target, allowing for the diameter of the bullet being constant at the different ranges and for the fact that the spread at 100yds and 100m is more than twice that at 50m. This had also been allowed for in the 1958 targets. Whereas the best rifle/ammunition combination may achieve 6 to 6.5mm centre to centre for ten shot groups and a good rifle/ammunition combination 8 to 8.5mm groups this is not the case at 100yds or 100m. The size of the groups cannot just be doubled as they may be up to half as much again. When the British targets were being developed for 100yds the multiplying factor was found to be 2.9.

The target used in international competitions and other important events at 50m has one aiming mark which therefore has to be changed frequently. Only one shot is fired at each aiming mark in all major competitions to avoid the problem of double shot holes and the difficulty of gauging them. These targets may be placed in a changer which brings the new target into view when the shooter presses a button. These changers may accept single targets in a stack or require a special fan fold pattern. An alternative method is for the target to be transported from the stopbutt to the firing

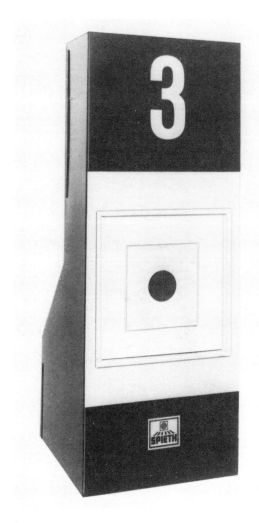

A very popular target changer which uses individual targets and presents a new one at the press of a button.

point where it can be changed either by the shooter or another person. Some ranges are equipped with pit marking just as in 300m or other big-bore ranges.

The system of target changers is expensive as many targets are used and in many domestic competitions more than one shot is fired at each aiming mark, or in systems where the shooter changes his own target by walking up to the frame and hanging a new target, multiple aiming marks are used. The three card system developed in the USA

The target transporters popular in Europe showing a target on its way back. The small wind flags are typical of those for UIT events.

is seen in some other English-speaking countries but rarely elsewhere. At 50m and 50yds there is usually one, sometimes two, sighting aiming marks at the top and four record or match aiming marks below. At 100m and 100yds there is only one sighting aiming mark and two record or match aiming marks below. A total of twenty shots are fired at each target to count for score – five on each at the shorter range and ten on each at the longer. Sighters are normally unlimited and the shooter is usually permitted to return to the sighter at any time even after the match shots have been commenced. This, of course, is prohibited under UIT rules unless the shooter through no fault of his own has a forced break of five minutes or longer when fresh unlimited sighters on one aiming mark are permitted.

There are pros and cons regarding the use of sighters after the match card has been started. It does mean that if you are

The target transporter which takes the target to and from the stopbutt.

35

Details of the motor and transporter.

accustomed to going back to the sighter you may not be prepared to judge the wind without first firing another sighter, and when you come to shoot under UIT rules you may find it difficult to continue in changing conditions without sighters after the match has started. However, those who shoot often under UIT rules do not so often return to the sighter even when permitted as they have more confidence in their wind doping ability.

At indoor ranges it is usual to print ten aiming marks on a target, one shot on each, as doubled shot holes are very common, particularly in the prone position. It is also common but not universal to have five aiming marks for kneeling and two for standing. The sighting target is sometimes incorporated on the main target but often attached to the frame, separate from the match target. Owing to the number of aiming marks and the naturally restricted size of the target card, there tends to be less white left around the aiming mark and therefore an artificially restricted size of frontsight aperture is used if the adjacent aiming marks are not to intrude or the sight picture is not to overrun the edge of the

card, when the background may not be the same colour or shade as the target. However, there is usually enough white to enable an acceptable frontsight size of 3.4 or 3.5mm to be chosen.

When the sighter is attached to the match target or adjacent, take care that the first shots do not end up on the match target in mistake for the sighter as this could be very detrimental to your score. It is very important that the sights are adjusted for the range in question for if there is insufficient elevation at the longer ranges, shots may well fall on or near the record aiming mark. Similarly, if there has been a lot of windage outdoors and you come to shoot indoors and forget to zero your sights, the first shot may clip the match target which could lose you ten points.

Outdoor targets and many indoor targets are gauged in the usual way, inwards, but the indoor targets used by Great Britain for 15, 20 and 25yds are gauged outwards. This means that the rings are designed so that the shot hole has to be entirely within the ring to score the higher value. If the shot hole touches the smallest ring, for example from the inside, it will score a nine. The outward gauge had to be adopted because the ten ring at 15yds would proportionately work out as a negative amount on inward gauging owing to the constant bullet diameter, irrespective of the range.

Until 1966 the air rifle target had a 2mm ten ring which was then changed to a target with a 1mm ten ring. From 1 January 1989 this was changed to a 0.5mm ten ring and although so small a size is difficult to print accurately, this is not so important as shot holes are gauged with a 5.5mm diameter gauge outwards. This is necessary as the pellet produces a maximum size hole and the 4.5mm gauge would tend to fall through, making accurate gauging difficult. The ten is therefore gauged out to the eight ring and the only time the normal gauge is used is for the one and two where there are no further rings out from which to gauge. The newest

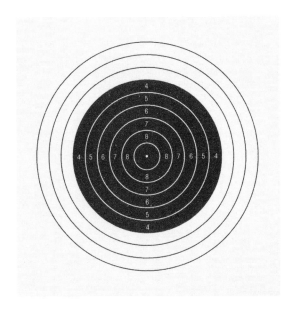

10m air rifle target.

target was calculated to give a maximum of 10.9 in the same way as the small-bore target when the target reading machine was used. Hence a 2.5mm wide ring gives $2.5 \times 2 - 4.5 = 0.5$mm.

Certainly scores had become very high with the 1mm target, especially amongst the women shooters, as has already been mentioned. The Finnish record for the 60 shot course for men was 599, although the world record stood at 597. All international shooting with the air rifle is standing and the only way to reduce scores acceptably and with certainty was to bring in a smaller target. Air rifles are certainly capable of putting all shots into the current ten ring with ease and again only time will tell if the reduction has been enough to last a reasonable length of time. If outward scoring were to be adopted then a ten ring of no value or a negative ten could result. This might be a solution for the future or for use as a good training target, when the normal target will appear to be that much easier, but

the shooter must not become complacent or scores will begin to suffer.

The target style used for all important competitions is one aiming mark on each target and one shot is shot at each to prevent any doubt over double shot holes. The paper used is a short fibre pattern which, when the pellet passes through, gives a clean round hole, almost like a wad cutter. It is permitted to have a larger plain card behind the target if a larger area of white around the aiming mark is desired, but not every shooter does this as many are quite happy with the standard size of card. The targets have to be changed for each shot and electric target changers are normally used which transport the target to and from the pellet catcher. A low-cost geared hand winder is also quite popular for use by the small club.

A practice target which is also used for some competitions has five aiming marks printed on a much larger card on which either one or two shots per aiming mark are shot. Not used in important competitions, this is nevertheless frequently seen when no target changers are in use and the shooter has to change the card or to have the card changed every five or ten shots.

The air rifle is also shot in a few countries at ranges shorter than the normal 10m and these targets are either proportioned to the 10m scoring rings to give similar scores or else, as in the case of the British 6yd target, are much easier. With the 6yd target good shooters frequently achieve scores close to the maximum and the very best shooters would not find it a challenge at all, but for the ordinary club with limited distances at which to shoot it can offer one solution. If a more difficult target were needed it would be a simple matter to convert the 10m target to outward gauging for use at the shorter distance, but this would make the scorer unhappy as the rings would be very close together!

4 Equipment

Although compared to some sports, rifle-shooting equipment appears to be fairly technical, the sport itself is not; it is a sport of the mind and body just like any other. So many shooters in the quest for improvement seek the erroneous way of added equipment, call them gadgets if you will because these are what much equipment becomes when used for this false purpose. The only way to improve scores is through training the mind and body, and no amount of equipment, no matter how advanced, will make a worthwhile improvement unless the mind and body are also given attention.

Much money is spent on the latest extra, instead of thinking before the money is spent. Of course a leading shooter needs good equipment, but, conversely, good equipment does not always make a leading shooter. Often it will be seen that the top shooter does not have the latest rifle, stock or device but is happy with the equipment that suits him. Constant change without thought is the easiest way to be side-tracked and wastes a lot of valuable time but once down that path it takes a determined person to go back and try the simpler route.

Well, what equipment is necessary? First to the clothing. What is worn under the shooting jacket poses no problems; a shirt or undershirt of cotton, not nylon as this slips, which fits well without binding and without folds that cause discomfort. A sweatshirt of sufficient thickness to help absorb pulsation but still within the maximum thickness permitted when measured with the other underclothing. Under UIT rules this is 2.5mm. Pants, again not of nylon and longjohns, particularly for the women as shooting trousers can be a little coarse. If the weather is going to be cold try thermal underwear – some specially made for shooting is available.

Choose a good *shooting jacket* from the start as this is probably the most important piece of equipment to buy; see what the leading shooters are using. Leather with its nice bright colours is fine and they do brighten up the ranges, but if cost is a factor choose canvas; leather coats are canvas lined anyway and canvas jackets can be just as good, even if they do not look so smart. Make sure that the jacket conforms to UIT rules and then it should conform to the national rules, but bear in mind that the reverse does not always apply. Be careful however that any canvas jacket is not too stiff and therefore outside the rules. If you are afraid that the jacket may not fit after a while and you are fully grown, then either exercise or go on to a sensible diet – better for you and your bank balance than buying new shooting clothing. Some people do have a weight problem or variation in weight and it is a point to think about.

If you are a junior who is still growing it is possible to buy junior jackets at reduced cost which are really quite good. If you are representing your country then you or more likely your parents may have to buy more than one shooting jacket and trousers during your junior years. It is important that the fit across the back is correct as support will be lost if the coat is able to move down the arms.

Trousers form the other large expenditure on shooting clothing and here perhaps canvas retains its designed stiffness better than leather. It is just as important to choose correctly not only for fit and appearance but also for the performance they give. See what the leading shooters are using. Like jackets

*A left-handed shooter with a canvas shooting jacket, not as colourful
as leather, but just as good.*

there are several good makes available but of
course do make sure that they accord to the
rules.

Shooting boots are necessary, otherwise
kneeling can be uncomfortable. Ensure that
they are the correct size and give support
where needed. Toes must not touch the
inside of the end of the boot when in
position, as this can be uncomfortable.
Ensure that the fastenings do not create a
problem or discomfort and try them on
whilst wearing the socks you intend to use.
These socks should not contain nylon and
should not be too thick or too thin. Most
modern shooting boots do not require thick
socks to protect you from the boots themselves as they are now well designed. Make
sure that they accord to the rules. The
kneeling cushion can be made of leather,
canvas or similar material and should be
filled with cork chippings, sawdust or similar
material which will retain its shape. Poly-

styrene is not suitable as it will crush when
the shooter's weight is on the cushion. There
must be a means of adding or removing the
filling so that the shooter can get it just right.

The *shooting hat* can be as colourful as you
wish as long as it is protective. On outdoor
ranges, or those not protected too well from
the sun, a long peak and side flaps are
necessary or a brim which can be bent to
suit. Remember you will have to wear ear-
muffs with your hat on, unless you have
specially-fitted plugs.

The other item of shooting clothing is the
glove, the type of which depends upon the
hand position standing. The five finger
pattern is the most flexible in this regard,
although the mitt or two or three fingered
glove may be preferred but gives less choice.
Whichever is chosen ensure that there is no
seam where the rifle rests and that the
fingers and thumb do not get constricted by
the end of the glove. The lining must not

bunch up and create a ridge and the outside should be of non-slip material in the palm and back. The glove must also conform to the rules.

The *sling*, which must be of the single point type, may be either of leather or plastic. Whichever material is chosen must not stretch and the plastic slings are now very popular. Choose a sling that will close sufficiently around the upper arm and preferably with a buckle adjustment which has the ability to be be moved out of the way so that it does not foul the trigger guard or the bottom of the forend. This can be a particular problem for shooters with short arms or those using a Standard Rifle with a deep forend. Not only is it illegal for the rifle to rest on the sling, but it may cause vertical variations in the group. Ensure that the sling can either be easily removed from the rifle or make a flat hook of the width of the sling swivel to facilitate attachment without struggling out of position.

Shooting spectacles will be covered in the section on aiming in Chapter 5.

A *shooting mat*, although not essential, is very desirable. Under UIT rules the mat has to be provided by the organisers and only these may be used, private mats are forbidden. However, in most national competitions you will have to provide your own shooting mat, so choose one that is of sufficient size to allow you to lie on it comfortably and with a non-slip portion for the elbows in the prone position. This area should be padded with a closed cell foam material which, although fairly firm and apparently unyielding to the elbows, will give comfortable support over a long period. Rather like German car seats – firm on first acquaintance but after many miles you can get up and walk away without any aches or pains! A soft mat is no use at all.

The *small-bore rifle*, a very important piece of equipment, in its various types, has already been described in Chapter 3. Buy

Victor Vlasov of the Soviet Union with the Free Rifle, prone. Note that a separate mat for the elbows is used and is often separate from the mat on which you lie.

the best you can; a really good second-hand rifle is better than a cheap new model. Do not overgun yourself – a Free Rifle does not have to be heavy and a lighter barrel might be better for you if you are lightly built, and it is capable of giving just the same results.

Ladies should buy a Standard Rifle even if your national rules allow you to use the Free Rifle. UIT rules demand that you use a Standard Rifle and many national competitions dictate its use. If you feel later that you want a Free Rifle or specialist prone rifle for national competitions buy one only after mastering the Standard Rifle. It is an easier rifle with which to shoot if used as intended and not laden with hook and palm rest. With men, costs may dictate that they buy only one small-bore rifle and that should naturally be the Free Rifle. Even so, try to learn to shoot with the Standard Rifle and then the adjustable buttplate and other accessories can be used as aids and not crutches.

The *air rifle* is simpler as there is only one basic style under the rules although the rifles are many and varied in concept. See what is most popular and what is winning the medals; a good indicator for all equipment is what is being used in the Olympic-type finals.

A *spotting telescope* and *stand* are essential for small-bore shooting, not only for seeing where your shots have gone but also to judge the wind. Whether it is angled or straight is a matter of personal preference. An angled telescope will need to be accurately placed, but when placed correctly offers less head movement and also has the advantage that it can be used on either the right or left of the shooting position. A straight telescope, although easier to place, may require some small head movement although many shooters would choose no other. Power only needs to be 20 to 25 times; anything more is not needed as the field of view is smaller and light transmission is less and there is no worthwhile advantage. Once the shot is fired you can do nothing about it and a higher

magnification has little purpose except that it may show you how close to the line the shot is.

The stand must be rigid and adjustable or adaptable to the heights required, and it must be stable at the greatest height at which it is going to be used with the telescope attached in the position desired. A bipod is convenient prone but may be less stable higher up unless of good quality. Some tripods have the legs arranged so that they do not interfere with the elbow in the prone position. Some of the more robust camera tripods are suitable for the standing position where there is no table or bench on which to rest the stand. A cover for the telescope is useful not only as protection but may also be used as a light shield if the flaps are standing up.

A *cartridge block* should be chosen which has room for 60 rounds plus a separate place for sighters. This is the most you will need in a match and any smaller number can of course be fitted in. It should have a lid to protect the ammunition and keep rubbish out and should be of a pattern whereby the holes can be easily cleaned as you do not want any debris or grit in these holes to find its way via the cartridge down your nice accurate barrel.

A good *stop-watch* is worth its weight in gold as many ranges do not have a clock within easy view and it is essential to be aware of the time remaining. Whether analogue or digital is a personal choice as is whether it shows the time elapsed or remaining.

Get a good *rifle case* of fibreboard, plastic or aluminium or similar with egg crate foam inside. Do not be tempted to cut this to the outline of the rifle as this is not what is intended; the rifle should lie in the foam and be held firmly. Cutting to the rifle outline may reduce the protection. A good strong case or bag for accessories will be needed to keep them together and protect them but eliminate anything unnecessary as a heavy bag will just cause fatigue.

5 The Three Positions

THE PRONE POSITION

The prone position is the steadiest commonly used position. Only the back position is steadier but this is not permitted under UIT rules and is now rarely seen except amongst the British long-range Match Rifle shooters who shoot from 1000 to 1200yds.

The position now adopted had seen little change until the mid 1980s when a variation on the established position was adopted by younger shooters from the USSR and East Germany and then spread, so that within a few years a number of shooters were using this new variation with success. However, it did not completely take over from the established position which continued to be taught in most countries.

First, the established position will be detailed and then the newer variation referred to. The established position is sometimes described as a modified Estonian position but the modern position is far removed from that used by the shooters from Estonia in the 1930s. The position used by them was noted for the body being at quite a wide angle, well rolled onto the left side, placing considerable weight onto the left elbow and the right leg being well drawn up and bent at the knee. Nobody would teach that position today, but in its time it was a marked advance.

The Established Position

The backbone of the prone position is the placing of the spine and this angle has tended to vary over the years. In 1955 it was near to thirty degrees, ten years later it was nearer twenty degrees and ten years beyond that twenty degrees was considered to be the

maximum while the minimum angle to the line of fire was only ten degrees. Naturally the angle will depend upon the build of the shooter – a tall shooter with long arms can lie at a much narrower angle than a shorter shooter with short arms. A small shooter lying at too narrow an angle will find his hands too close together giving a very short base, even when the butt is considerably

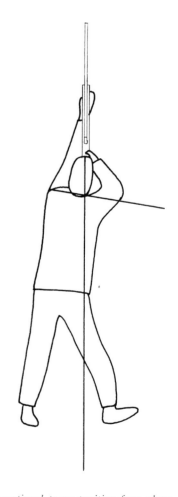

The conventional prone position from above.

42

Prone with the Standard Rifle from the right side; eye looks straight ahead, cheekpiece is packed up to provide support for the head. The sling buckle, although clear of the forend, can on some slings be adjusted out of the way. Sally Waters has won both the British Ladies 3 × 20 and the Air Rifle Championships.

shortened. Therefore an angle of between five and twenty degrees, depending upon build, is sensible. Even so a few shooters may still find it necessary to exceed the maximum angle to achieve a reasonable distance apart for the hands. To go beyond twenty degrees, unless absolutely necessary because of small stature, means that the butt of the rifle is toward the outside of the position and the line of recoil moved too far from the centre which is therefore less easily controlled. Additionally, it is less easy to achieve a good head position and good working conditions for the eyes.

Once the angle to the line of fire has been established, make sure that the spine is kept as nature intended, i.e. straight with the shoulders square to the spine, not like a banana. This usually occurs when a shooter has heard that one should lie straighter but

hasn't thought the whole position through. Often the legs and hips are moved but not the shoulders, which is often aggravated by a butt that is too long and/or a left hand that is too far along the forend. Many young shooters use a rifle that is too long in the butt and they may well be forced into a bad position from the start. This is difficult to eradicate as they have to unlearn the old position before the new position becomes natural to them. Certainly it is difficult to see oneself in the prone position but video cameras can be a useful aid to correcting one's position when prone.

The left leg should be positioned approximately parallel to the spine with the left foot resting on the toe or alternatively turned inwards. Do not turn the left foot outwards as this is a strained position. If used, the extension sole on the shooting boots may be

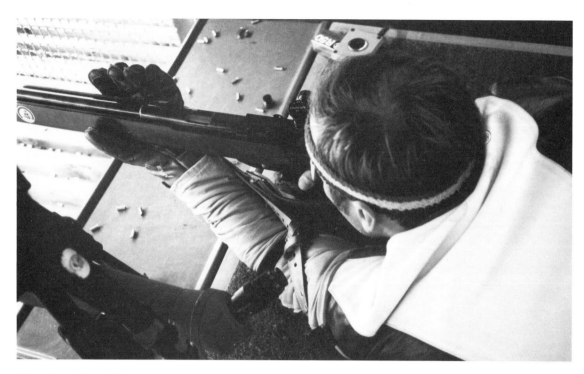

Prone from above, left hand not too far forward in a good position and the left elbow to the left of the rifle. Angled telescope not normally this far away.

Prone right side; a good position, right first (trigger) finger clear of the stock, left hand in good position, not too far forward. Neil Braisher has won the Earl Roberts trophy for the British small-bore prone Championship three times. He is tall and has extended the butt of the Free Rifle, keeps his right wrist straight and is using a hook buttplate as do most Free Rifle shooters in the prone position.

Isabelle Heberle of France prone from a table. If it is questioned why the shooter does not use this side of the table, look at the leg position in the bottom right photograph.

Neil Braisher from in front, elbow to the left of the rifle, upright head and moderate cant. He is using a spirit level on his Free Rifle.

Isabelle Heberle makes the best use of the table with an almost ideal right leg position. Normal position of feet, right flat, left on toe.

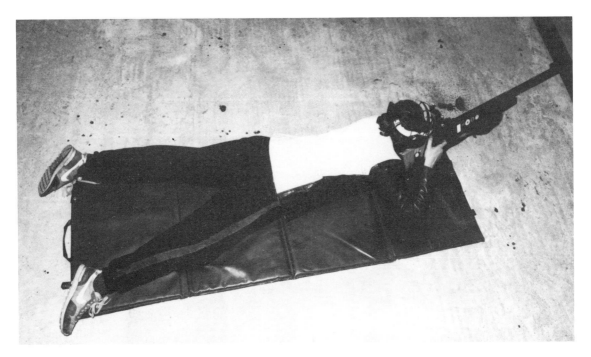

No strain, no 'banana', the normal prone position.

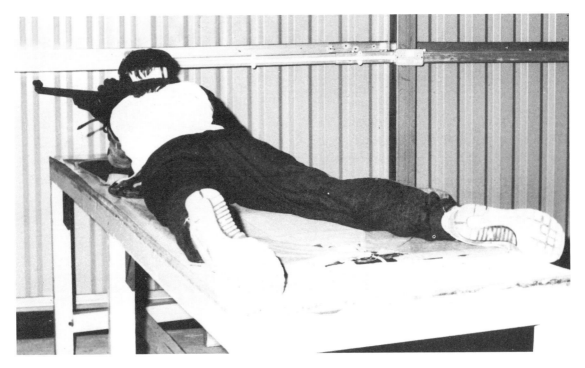

Viewed from behind; left arm, the spine and left leg in line.

cut at an angle so that the left foot rests securely, although many shooters use trainers and find no problem.

The right leg has more variation, but do not copy the position your favourite shooter uses as he may use it for some particular reason or be built differently. The thigh should be angled at forty-five to sixty degrees from the spine with a very slight bend at the knee to allow the lower leg to rest comfortably. This slight bend is needed, as with the thigh at this angle it will raise the right side of the pelvis and the thigh will be pointing downwards. Without that slight bend the lower leg would have to continue underground or in a very uncomfortable position. If the firing points are crowded or one is shooting from tables it may be necessary to bend the leg at the knee until one stays in the available space or on the table. The right foot should be placed flat pointing outwards. The position of the right leg is not critical providing it remains consistent and a few degrees one way or the other makes very little difference except perhaps to comfort. If it is necessary to change the normal position of the right leg at any time do make sure that you have learnt beforehand what, if anything, will happen to your hold pattern and your zero.

You will now find that the body is rolled to the left which makes breathing easier and reduces pulsation. However, it is nowhere near to the Estonian position nor is strain placed on the left elbow. The UIT and most countries demand that the left forearm must not be less than thirty degrees from the horizontal. Below this angle is permissible in some countries but not internationally, nor is a very low position desirable or as stable. Additionally you do not want the range officers or jury hovering around you because you are below the permitted limit. The left arm is drawn forward, but not excessively, to give a reasonable base. When viewed from above the upper arm and forearm should be in a straight line. This will place the elbow to the left of the rifle which is correct. Do not place the elbow under the rifle as this will have the effect of breaking the elbow joint and the support from the sling will be lost. There will then be a tendency to keep on tightening the sling which will draw the left hand and wrist back toward the upper arm and give a very strained position. Additionally, with the elbow under the rifle it will tend to recoil to the left instead of straight back. Remember that the arm should be straight when viewed from above, so do not push the elbow to the left or right but leave it in its natural position.

The forend should rest across the base of the hand which should be held open and the fingers should not grip the stock or touch the

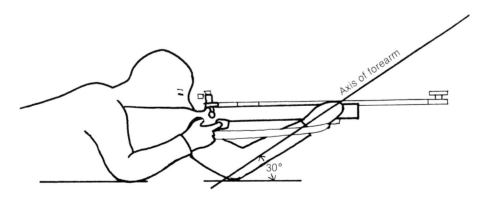

Prone position. Note that the 30 degree angle is from axis of forearm to the horizintal – not the firing point.

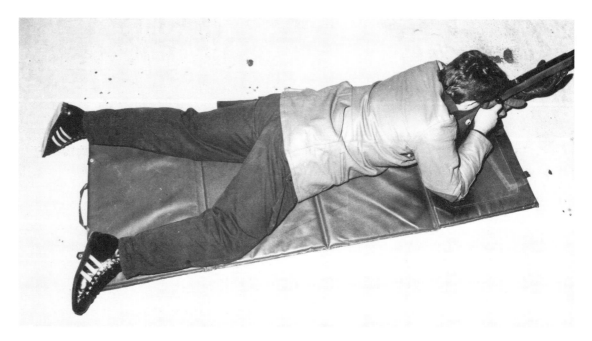

Prone by a more substantially built shooter, right knee drawn up more.

A very high, straight prone position; the right knee drawn up almost at right angles can just be seen.

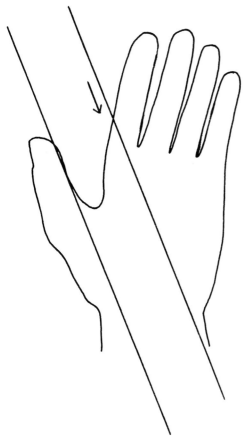

Position of forend on hand. Angled handstop would cause pressure at arrow, therefore round or slightly shaped handstop fits fleshy area to left of arrow.

barrel. If the forend is placed too far out on the palm, the wrist can bend, whilst too far to the left may well transmit a pulse and give an uncomfortable position for the thumb. The handstop should be round, approximately 25 to 40mm in diameter or with a slight shaping and this will allow it to fit into the fleshy part of the hand between thumb and forefinger. The old angled handstops which are still seen today should either be modified or consigned to a museum! The forend channel, into which the accessories fit, should be filled with the appropriate strip to avoid discomfort. If the factory strip appears to be too long do not be afraid of cutting it.

The right elbow should be placed naturally with the right shoulder slightly higher than the left. The right side will be raised anyway by the position of the right leg and pelvis and the shoulder should lie naturally square to the spine. The right hand should be a continuation of the forearm without the bent wrist so often seen. The hand does not need to be tucked in behind the pistol grip as this will inhibit the operation of the trigger finger. The hand held naturally gives the best position for the trigger finger to function efficiently. The right arm does not act as an additional support for the rifle, but merely takes the hand to the pistol grip and the finger to the trigger. The right arm must be relaxed.

The head must be kept as upright as possible, first to enable the vestibular organs – the organs of balance – to function correctly and secondly so that the eyes may look straight out of their sockets to give them the best possibility to see efficiently without distortion. The eyes should not be looking across the bridge of the nose. The buttplate rests on the upper right chest, commonly called in the shoulder, in the region of the pectoralis major and the deltoid muscles; this means that the rifle is to the right of the aiming eye. Do not tilt the head to the rifle as the vestibular organs in the ear of the tilted head will respond and create movement trying to restore the balance; hold pattern will be increased and become irregular. It is almost impossible to achieve the perfect head position and at best the eyes will be looking slightly toward the left, but every effort should be made to achieve as good a head position as possible.

The head should not be tilted toward the stock but there are alternatives. It is unlikely that with an upright head and an upright rifle you will be able to see through the sights. One alternative is to cast off the stock, in other words to have the buttplate, or with a target rifle preferably to have the whole butt, moved to the right of the centre line. This can be very expensive and may

Good head position, rifle canted to head, both eyes open. It can be seen that the elbow is to the left of the rifle, not beneath.

Good head position; no need to worry about the 30° rule, well clear.

not be entirely the solution. Another alternative is to offset the sights, which is still popular on 300m rifles, but this does have the disadvantage that the rifle is moved further from the centre of the position. The third alternative is to cant the rifle, which is simply to rotate the rifle until the sights are in such a position that they are in front of the eye. Bringing the rifle to the eye is the method adopted by the majority of shooters. The angle of cant, as it is called, will vary from one person to another depending on build. Although the sights are no longer upright and the windage and elevation no longer true, this is less important than the necessity of keeping a good head position. In fact windage is seldom needed at exactly nine or three o'clock as the effect of the wind on the rotating bullet also necessitates some elevation change, unless only a very small change is required. To a left-handed shooter this cant may be an advantage in a wind as the angle of cant may well lie nearly along the line at which the wind deflects the bullet, and the windage adjustment may indeed be spot on. It is just as important to keep the rifle at the same angle as it would be to keep it upright. It is no more difficult to keep cant constant than it is easier to keep the rifle upright. To facilitate either, a spirit level may be used, except in Standard Rifle events where it is not permissible. However, lugs can be filed on the frontsight insert so that it may be rotated, or in some frontsights rotation is possible in the frontsight itself. Bars may be used with a transparent aperture, either independently or even cut from a metallic insert. Cant will also be dealt with more fully later as it is important.

Ensure that the head is rested on the cheekpiece in exactly the same manner every time. If there is any variation, recoil will alter causing a misplacement of the shot. The head position must not vary during the shoot, either in its position or in the weight placed on the stock. The modern angular cheekpieces are to be preferred rather than the older rounded pattern. The butt should

be placed as close to the neck as it can be to keep the rifle as close to the centre of the position as possible and avoid any added difficulty with the head. The heel of the butt may either be placed in the pocket below the collarbone or on the bone itself. The Free Rifle hook buttplate will almost certainly rest on the collarbone. The buttplate must always be in the same position as any variation will have a marked effect on the fall of the shot. It is very easy to vary its position without really being aware of a small variation. If the hook is used it must be offset so that the rifle comes in as close to the neck as possible whilst the hook passes under the arm; the hook has an added advantage in that it allows more consistent placement or replacement of the buttplate in the shoulder. For a starting position the bottom of the hook buttplate base needs offsetting about one centimetre more to the right than the top; offset will vary according to build and slightly more or less may be necessary. If a conventional buttplate is used this should be raised, but remember the legal limit on a Standard Rifle.

The butt should be of such a length that the right arm is not cramped, nor should it be necessary to stretch to the pistol grip, and the right hand should fall naturally onto the grip. Most stocks are adjustable in length but if it is too long do not be afraid to cut the stock. Measure twice and cut once is good advice and if uncertain seek help. The pistol grip should be held with moderate pressure, enough to lift a full wet milk bottle. The trigger finger must be free of the stock so if there is a little wood in the way, shave it off. To increase pressure of the butt in the shoulder move the handstop or sling swivel forward a small amount, say 1cm, but ensure that it does not move the shoulder rearward.

In the newer variation referred to earlier, the spine is still straight but the pelvis is rotated, the right side being much higher than in the established position and there is little or no contact with the ground between

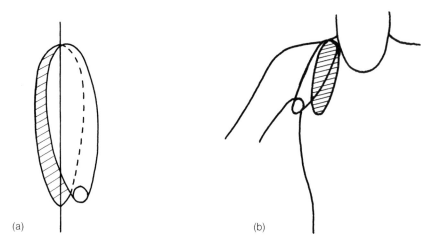

(a) The logical start for Free Rifle buttplate lateral and adjustment (looking toward muzzle) (b) Free Rifle buttplate angled so that hook is under arm and butt as close to neck as possible.

the left inner thigh and the right knee. The left leg is more nearly parallel to the line of fire and the foot is turned inwards. The right lower leg is bent more at the knee and the right foot is therefore closer to the left leg than with the established position. Because the body tends to be rolled more to the left the elbow is slightly less to the left of the rifle and the left hand is consequently somewhat further forward on the forend. A good feature of this variation is that the line of the recoil is almost directly between the feet and very close to the centre of the position. It has been said that shooters using this position are copying Gennadi Lushikov of the USSR, but the amount of cant which he employs is not carried over. He cants at some thirty-five degrees even when using the 300m Free Rifle with offset sights. He is one of the world's finest and most consistent rifle shooters and interestingly in other positions he cants only a normal amount. Other shooters using a similar position cant in the normal manner. Only time will tell whether this newer variation will prove a breakthrough or an important variation used with success by some shooters. It certainly

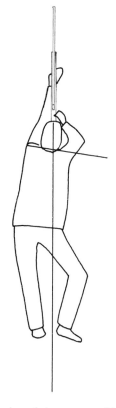

The new variation of the prone position from above.

Gennardi Lushikov from behind – the first shooter to use the new prone position variation.

produces very good results but whether it will be better for every shooter is uncertain.

The handstop or sling swivel, whichever is used, must be so placed that it fits snugly against the glove of the left hand when the shooter is in position and the clothing and shoulder pad compressed as if the rifle was firmly in the shoulder. It is only at this stage that the sling should be introduced; do not try and struggle with adjustments to the position with the sling attached. The sling must be of the single point type, as the two point type is inferior in every respect except for carrying the rifle, and should be placed either high or low on the upper left arm to avoid pulsation from the brachial artery. It should pull from the outside of the arm and be supported by a strap or similar device

attached to the shooting coat to stop it from sliding down the arm. It should not be so tight that blood circulation is restricted and with a strap to prevent it sliding there is no need for this. The high sling position is favoured by most shooters as giving optimum support, but a few successful shooters prefer the low position. The sling should pass across the back of the wrist and hand and only be tight enough to prevent the left hand dropping from the weight of the rifle. It should support the weight of the rifle but should not be so tight as to cause pulsation and strain. Use a wide flat hook that fits the sling swivel to prevent any variation in placement of the sling in the swivel, unless the swivel is easily removable with the sling. The sling should be attached as close to the left hand or handstop as possible, not a long way forward up the forend away from the left hand.

A good shooting glove must be used to protect the hand from the pressure of the sling and handstop or swivel. There should be no seam where the rifle rests and the fingers of the glove must be long enough that no pressure is applied to the fingertips when in position. So-called summer gloves may not be desirable on open ranges as hot sun on the exposed fingertips can be quite painful.

The height of the cheekpiece is important and if this is not adjustable some taping or removal of wood may be necessary. Similarly the thickness may be either too thick or too thin for the individual. One way to determine the correct fit of the cheekpiece is to shoot a group with the rearsight removed. The group should be centred in the nine ring at six o'clock but note that the group will be low when the cheekpiece is correct when no rearsight is used. If the group is too low the cheekpiece is too low, if high the cheekpiece is too high, if to the left too thick, if to the right too thin. Of course it will most likely be a combination of these. The eye is the rearsight but care should be exercised that the amount of cant is correct. With the aid

Prone from the left side, sling well-supported.

Barry Dagger shows an interesting variation in that the sling is not attached close to the handstop but a little way in front, so that he finds that he can adjust the handstop independently.

of another shooter or a mirror you can see if the cant is correct, but remove the bolt or action first, remembering at all times that safety is most important. If you have an adjustable or removable cheekpiece, the original can be replaced with a piece of wood so that it can be experimented upon before reshaping or replacing the original. There is also the advantage that if you do not get it correct the first time, you can start all over again. If it is not removable, try taping the cheekpiece or if it is too high, first try a higher frontsight block before cutting the wood. Go slowly and carefully especially on any lateral error unless you are certain your angle of cant is correct.

Once you have the cheekpiece correct it will be correct for only one range but as the indoor ranges and 50m are only some 2½ minutes apart this is not such a big problem as the difference between 50m and 100yds. Either use the adjustable cheekpiece or use a two step frontsight block or two heights of frontsight. Many shooters ensure that the cheekpiece is correct for 50m and let the other ranges take care of themselves as they feel that 50m is the most important for them. Then extra care is needed to centre the eye in the rearsight aperture at 100yds and there is enough to think about already. The rearsight aperture should be some 40mm from the eye, although further away is acceptable, and it should appear to be approximately 1.5 times the diameter of the frontsight tunnel. The distance from the eye will be one of the variables in choosing the size of rear aperture used; this may be in the region of 1 to 1.2mm although the majority may well use 1.1mm.

When reloading in the prone position it is better to lift the right elbow from the ground, open the bolt, pick up the cartridge, insert the cartridge fully into the chamber – push it in all the way – close the bolt gently

Reload by lifting the right elbow.

A low but legal prone position, shooting from the top of the a table.

and replace the elbow on the ground. Whilst doing this, avoid undue movement of the shoulder as any movement forward only moves the rifle away from the hand that is trying to reload. When reloading it does not matter if the butt is taken out of the shoulder each time, it just needs care to replace it in exactly the same place each and every time. Hold the butt by picking it up at the toe and not the pistol grip; this enables easier and more accurate placement. Do not reload by rolling the position to the right as this can change the position and additional movement is needed to come back into the correct position. Reloading quickly can save valuable time, but never be at the expense of follow through which must be maintained until well after the bullet has passed through the target.

To orientate the position, aim, then close the eyes, relax, stop breathing, open the eyes and look at the position of the sights relative to the target. If they are to the right or left move the body around the left elbow. If the rifle is slightly high move the body forward a little without moving the elbows and if low move the body back a little. This is for minor alterations only, or for alterations of position owing to a need on multi-aiming mark targets. Any major alteration owing to position error must be analysed and corrected. When using multi-aiming mark targets either indoor or outdoor do not be complacent and merely push the rifle from one aiming mark to another as poor results will occur and you will only have yourself to blame. If you take care and do the job properly, the results will be your reward.

THE STANDING POSITION

The standing position is the least stable of the three classic positions owing to its high centre of gravity and small support area. Even so, scores are now very high and indeed increasing; it is not uncommon to see a score of 100 in a ten shot series at 50m and scores of 390 plus for 40 shots are being achieved. In the air rifle event, which internationally is shot only in the standing position, scores are now such that only one point or at most very few, are being dropped for the whole match. Who would have thought that a few years ago?

To adopt the standing position the shooter should stand ninety degrees from the target, although a slightly smaller angle may suit some shooters. Much of the weight of the rifle is well in front of the shooter and to counterbalance this mass it is necessary to adopt a position which is far from upright, otherwise the muscles would be under considerable strain. To place the least strain on the muscles, which would rapidly tire, the shooter has to use his bones and ligaments to best advantage. Women have a certain advantage in the standing position owing to their lower centre of gravity, a more prominent, higher iliac ridge and often a shorter waist than the men.

Imagine if a rifle were handed to you so that it was cradled in your arms, it would be necessary to bend the back and throw the hips forward to take the weight. Any attempt to stand upright whilst cradling this weight in the arms would bring on rapid fatigue. This is the first step to be taken in adopting the position. However, with the rifle in a shooting position and the buttplate against the shoulder there is still a large distance between the buttplate and the centre of gravity or point of balance of the rifle. It is necessary then not only to bend the back and throw the hips forward but also to bend the body to the side. This brings the mass of the rifle nearer to the shooter but the point of balance will almost certainly still be outside of the support area, the feet. To achieve still greater rigidity in the small of the back, the

Right side close-up, standing; palm rest on base of hand, thumb to the left as seen in left side view, upper arm supported against body.

Left side standing, feet about shoulder-width apart, left arm forward of vertical.

Standing right side. Good overall position by slim shooter, note sight raising blocks as shooter has longish neck.

Left side close-up standing: Note palm rest, left hand, and right hand; eye relief moderate.

upper body is turned some fifteen degrees to the left which will then provide this additional support. When first adopting this position some discomfort may well be felt in the small of the back, but this will disappear as the shooter becomes accustomed to the position.

The support area comprises the feet which should be placed about shoulder width apart. For a stocky shooter the feet may be somewhat further apart than for a tall thin shooter. In recent years the feet have tended to be slightly further apart than formerly. The feet are placed comfortably with the toes slightly further apart than the heels which enables the muscles in the legs to control the position better. The weight should be distributed evenly on both feet with the weight slightly nearer the balls of the feet than the heels. Tension in the knee joints is

important; these should be tensed as if you were talking to somebody important, too tense and the muscles tire early and the tension will cause poor stability, too slack and body movement will occur. The lower part of the body is the active part and controls the position, whilst the upper part of the body is the passive part. The earlier popular position of standing with one leg straight and the other knee bent has been largely superseded, although there are still a few shooters using that position.

The left arm supports the rifle and the elbow should be rested on the front of the hip-bone or a little to the right, on the stomach muscle. If the arm is insufficiently long to reach the hip bone or the shooter is long waisted do not worry for the arm can be rested on the chest which gives excellent support. Do not position the arm too far

Standing, from the front: elbow under rifle, upright head, some cant. However, right hip is a little too far forward to be ideal, but still acceptable.

Standing, from rear; Free Rifle buttplate adjusted so that stock is as close to head as possible, right arm free.

across the chest towards the heart area or an unwanted pulse may be transmitted. When viewed from the side the forearm should be near vertical without cramping the elbow joint and when viewed from in front the elbow should be beneath the rifle.

With the Standard Rifle and the air rifle a palm rest is not permitted but these rifles usually have a deeper forend which can be rested on the left hand in a number of ways. Many women and a few men rest the forend on the closed fist with the weight mainly on the backs of the first and second fingers. If this provides insufficient height it is possible to place the forend preferably between the second and third fingers with the thumb either on the forend or under the trigger guard, or, if that is too uncomfortable, between the first and second fingers. There

are a great many varieties of position to be seen, but do not place the rifle on the top of outstretched fingers as these have too many joints and the hand will rapidly tire, giving poor results.

With the Free Rifle a palm rest may be used, which is merely a downward extension of the forend to allow for insufficient length of arms. It enables the rifle to be raised to give a better head position and although in the early 1980s it looked as if the palm rest was losing favour, some five years later it was gaining popularity again. The palm rest should be placed on the base of the hand, not on the fingers, transmitting the weight backward and pressing the upper arm against the chest. With many shooters the left hand presses slightly forward on the palm rest, the forward movement being

Close-up of hand position, between second and third fingers.

An alternative hand position.

arrested by the knob or angle on the hook buttplate. Usually the thumb is to the left. A wide variety of palm rests may be seen, from a simple block of wood to quite elaborate affairs.

The buttplate rests lightly against the shoulder joint and not on the upper right chest as with the other positions. There is not the shoulder pressure as with prone and kneeling, and the whole position tends to be relaxed down and forward along the line of the left upper arm and shoulder/buttplate contact. Some shooters do, however, exert a slight rearward pull. With the Standard Rifle the buttplate should be moved downward to raise the rifle and give a better head position. With the Free Rifle the buttplate should also be adjusted downward but also laterally to place the hook under the arm and the butt as close into the neck as possible to avoid having to move the head to the rifle. As with the prone position, the

(Above)   An alternative hand position if the arms are long enough, and often used by women shooters.

(Left)   Standing right side. Elbow reaches hip, more back bend necessary with this lighter-weight shooter.

Close-up of the upper body from in front.

bottom of the buttplate should be moved out in the same direction but somewhat more than the top. This should reduce the angle of cant although some cant will almost certainly be necessary. Always remember to bring the rifle to the head and not the other way around in order to give the best possible conditions for the organs of balance and for the eyes to do their job efficiently. The head should also not be drawn back or craned forward. The rearsight may be adjusted rearwards but eye relief may well be greater than in the prone position so choose a rear aperture to suit and to give a similar sight picture. Owing to the natural uprightness of the head in this position a very good sight picture can be achieved.

The right arm is held free from the body and at a comfortable angle. The hand should

Standing left side with the Standard Rifle.

Standing, from in front; head upright, rifle canted to head.

hold the pistol grip in the same way as in the other positions without influencing the rifle. The area of the right shoulder and arm must be relaxed, but ensure that the angle of the arm is kept constant. Do not believe that because the standing position is less steady than prone or kneeling that a lighter trigger weight is indicated. Just the reverse is true in fact, it is possible to get away with a fairly light trigger prone but not in the standing position when it is all too easy to let off a shot when the hold is not quite ready. But more of that later when we cover triggers and trigger control.

To orientate the position if the rifle is to the left or right, move the whole position as if on a turntable. If the rifle is too low raise the palm rest on the Free Rifle or move the hand slightly rearward on the Standard or air rifle. With the sloping forend seen on many

Standing, from behind.

of these rifles only a small movement will make a considerable difference at the target. Conversely, to lower the rifle, lower the palm rest or move the hand slightly forward, on the Standard Rifle or air rifle. Small movements may also be made by adjusting the buttplate. Remember that these alterations are for small movements only – do not under any circumstances alter the back bend as this will upset the whole position. Any big movements will usually be because of an incorrect position and this needs to be re-established first before any necessary small alterations are made.

It is important to choose good footwear as run-down shoes or boots will give little stability either on the ground or to the feet in them. The modern shooting trousers which were originally developed to give comfort in the kneeling position are now used in the standing position to give support

to the back, whilst the old-fashioned shooting coat with its large bulky pre-shaped pads is not at all helpful for standing.

It is not essential to have a Free Rifle to be able to shoot small-bore standing; under the UIT rules the ladies have to use the Standard Rifle, and in the ladies event and the 300m Standard Rifle scores equal to those shot with the Free Rifle are seen, additionally the 300m Standard Rifle requires a minimum trigger weight of 1500gm. It is better to start standing with a Standard Rifle or air rifle and then graduate to the Free Rifle. The palm rest and adjustable hook buttplate may then be used as aids and not as crutches by those with poor position or technique.

It is particularly important when shooting standing as a beginner that a sufficiently large front sight insert is used to contain all normal movement. The aiming mark should not 'bounce' against the inside of the aperture as this will cause tensing and consequent poor results. It may be advantageous to consider a blade or post frontsight as it gives only one point of aim and quicker awareness of movement.

To reload in the standing position it is necessary to rest the rifle after each shot as it is not practical to remain in aim for long periods. This can be done by placing the rifle on the table or platform provided or resting the butt on a chair, but take care where the muzzle points. However both these methods require lifting the rifle some distance each time it is replaced in the shoulder. An alternative method is to have a high rest either on a platform or secure adapted telescope stand, then the butt can be left in the shoulder and the forend rested on this high rest only a short distance away. The ammunition can be placed in a similar high position or in any other handy place that does not involve stretching or reaching.

When shooting with the air rifle it is sensible to adopt a sequence of events as many of them, especially those that precompress the air, require some effort to cock.

Close-up of upper body with the air rifle. Note that cheekpiece has been raised to support the head, and that the lens of the shooting glasses is square to the line of sight.

Isabelle Heberle standing shows a conventional position and also shows that with a Standard Rifle the stock can be made to suit within the rules – it does not have to be as made by the factory that made the rifle.

Vesela Letcheva of Bulgaria uses the position where the weight is mainly on the left leg and the right one is bent at the knee. She uses it with great success.

Vesela Letcheva shows clearly the bent right leg.

DDR shooter who places the right foot slightly to the rear of the left foot.

Close-up of right and left hands standing. Note that the right wrist is straight, not tucked in, behind pistol grip and left hand is a variation in that it is turned to the left.

Standing, from rear. Note adjustment of buttplate and rifle canted to the head. Even with the Standard Rifle the butt is well in toward the head and neck with only a minimal gap.

Close-up of hand position from in front to show how the fingers are 'split'.

Malcolm Foskett, a more substantially built shooter, needs less back bend than the lighter shooter. The weight transferred in the back bend is greater.

Malcolm Foskett's left elbow does not reach the hip-bone but adequate support is taken from the chest against which the upper arm rests.

Carmen Giese of West Germany has her feet apart more than normal,
but it works well for her.

Carmen Giese from the back.

Eva Forian of Hungary stands squarer to the target than normal but this variation works well for her too.

Loading the air rifle using a chair.

After the preceding shot has been released, cock the rifle, bring back the target, replace the target and return the target to the stopbutt. Most ranges have electric target changers but some still have hand-operated changers which require a little effort to use. After the target has been returned then load the next pellet, and be ready for the next shot. As with the small-bore rifle, do remember to load carefully and the same each time with the pellet to the same depth and without damaging it and you will find that better results will be obtained.

When adopting the standing position, the back bend and bend of the body to the side comes first; the rifle may then be mounted and the upper body then rotated the fifteen degrees or whatever similar angle is adopted. Move the upper body a little past the normal position to the left and then back so that a natural place is found from which to orientate the position.

THE KNEELING POSITION

The kneeling position has two basic positions, the high and the low. The high utilises the kneeling cushion whilst the low does not and the shooter sits on the side of the right foot. The choice of the basic position depends not only on body conformation but also on whether it is possible for the shooter, even with training, to sit on the side of the right foot for lengthy periods. The low position is not often seen although the great Olympic and World Champion Gary Anderson, towards the end of his international shooting career, experimented with

Alister Allan of Great Britain and Scotland, the first man to shoot 600 prone on the 1958 targets at a major International and thus gain the World Record, and Olympic record holder in the 3 × 40 event 1988, scoring 1181.

the low kneeling position and his results improved considerably. Kneeling then went from his weakest position to one of consistent strength. The body conformation to take advantage of the low position is one with a long trunk and relatively short arms. In this case the use of a kneeling roll would only raise the trunk further, to the detriment of the position. However, even if a shooter has this body conformation and cannot sit on the side of the foot, then it is pointless adopting the low position.

The kneeling roll or cushion consists of a bag with maximum dimensions of 25cm long and 18cm diameter and it is placed beneath the right instep. It should be filled with sawdust, cork chippings or other similar material which will support the shooter's weight without collapsing. It is not advisable therefore to use a filling such as polystyrene chips which deform and lose their shape. The kneeling roll supports the weight of the right leg and body and must be comfortable and supportive and not too tightly packed, which will be too hard and unyielding and give too small an area of contact. Remember that these are maximum dimensions and it is not necessary in most cases to be anywhere close to them in diameter. When knelt over, the kneeling roll will be compressed to a smaller or greater extent in the centre.

The shooter shoots out of the position, facing towards the target much as in the prone position, with the shoulders some seventy to seventy-five degrees to the line of

Overall view of kneeling from right. Note position of right leg, left elbow, body rolled forward but still over support area.

Overall view of kneeling from left; left leg near vertical, spine rolled.

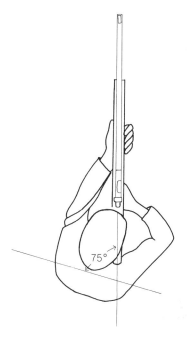

Kneeling from the front; elbow to shooter's left of rifle, upright head and moderate cant.

Kneeling position from above. Note shoulder angle to line of fire.

Close-up of kneeling cushion or roll.

The kneeling position from behind; note foot is opened out and kneeling cushion is shallow.

shooter leans forward and the amount the shoulders are rolled forward, the majority of the weight still being over the support area of the right foot and a small variation in the amount carried by the left leg, which is mainly the left arm and upper body. The right foot is opened out and placed across the kneeling roll with the footwear chosen of such size that the foot hangs freely within the boot without the toe actually touching the end, so the weight is therefore taken through the boot and the kneeling roll to the floor and not via the toes. The fastening of the right boot should be loosened for comfort and the foot when viewed from the rear should be vertical or nearly so. The spine should be placed centrally on the right heel or with the foot slightly to the right if the former is uncomfortable. It is sensible to wear either proper shooting trousers or at least use reinforcements according to the rules to make the position more comfortable. The right leg should be placed at a natural angle and it will be found when the position has been correctly adopted that it is possible to raise the right knee from the ground with little effort as so little weight is placed on that knee.

The left leg is placed about one half step forward with the shin near to vertical. The left foot is turned comfortably inward but not excessively so as this would only cause strain and would not increase stability. The fastening of the left boot should remain tight

fire. Having the shoulders along the line of fire will produce an unstable position. The right leg is placed at an angle of approximately sixty to sixty-five degrees to the line of fire and the left foot is placed in a comfortable position some thirty to forty-five degrees to the line of fire. It should be remembered that these angles are not inviolable and that in the kneeling position body conformation plays a bigger part in position differences than either prone or standing. The right heel and the roll support the majority of the weight with the left leg being comparatively lightly loaded and very little weight on the right knee. Therefore the weight distribution is very much toward the left side of the position, with the mass when viewed from the front being close to the line of the left heel.

The weight distribution when viewed from the side will depend on the amount the

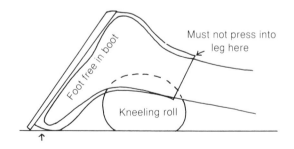

The foot kneeling does not touch the inside of the end of the boot. The weight is taken through the boot and the kneeling roll.

but certainly not so tight that circulation is restricted. The body should lean forward slightly and the head and shoulders rolled forward; the spine will then carry the major part of the weight of the upper body, relieving the muscles of the work. By varying the amount of the slight forward lean and the rolling of the shoulders it is possible to find a position in which the horizontal movement is minimised as much as possible.

For most beginners this sideways movement poses the biggest problem but it must be stressed that the majority of the body weight is still over the main support area, the right foot and roll. The left elbow should rest on the left knee with the elbow in the hollow of the knee which seems especially designed for it! However, if body conformation is such that this placing is impossible it may be placed either forward or to the rear of the knee with the rules stipulating a maximum of 100mm in front of and 150mm behind the point of the knee. The left leg and elbow should be to the left of the rifle, the elbow being somewhat more to the left than in the prone position. Any attempt to place the elbow beneath the rifle will mean that the left arm is turned inward and the muscles of the shoulder will be in a poor condition and again the horizontal movement will be increased. When viewed from above the left arm should be in a straight line and not 'broken' at the elbow, again similar to prone. The weight should be taken directly down through the left leg without any tendency for the leg to be moved to the left or right. When viewed from the front the left shin is vertical.

The rifle is placed as close to the neck as

This shooter rolls the body more, being further forward.

Trouser zipper opened to prevent bunching of material behind the knee and help circulation.

possible and the buttplate will usually be adjusted downwards to raise the rifle so as to give as good a head position as you can without having to tilt the head down excessively. The buttplate on the Free Rifle is adjusted laterally as in the prone position but is somewhat shorter in length. Although a better head position is possible when kneeling than when prone, it will almost certainly be necessary to cant the rifle and do remember always to bring the rifle to the head and not vice versa. Avoid any sideways tilting of the head as much as possible as this will induce sway when the vestibular organs indicate an imbalance. It is also necessary to ensure that the eyes are in the best position in which to do their job. The left hand is held as in the prone position and the forend rests on the base of the hand and not out on the palm. Without the sling and with the rifle rested on the left hand, try variations on the rolling of the shoulders to see if these minor variations produce a more stable position, with particular attention to any sideways or horizontal movement.

The right arm plays little part in the position and should be relaxed with the elbow held just above a fully-dropped position; the pistol grip should be held as in prone without any bend at the wrist and the trigger finger free of the woodwork of the stock. It may well be found once a correct position has been adopted that it is remarkably stable even without the sling, therefore once the handstop or sling swivel has been positioned against the glove of the left hand with the rifle approximately horizontal attach the sling in the same

Kneeling from in front; upright head, rifle canted to head. Shooting coat opened for lower half.

manner as prone, and again not too tightly. The sling is not used to prevent blood circulation but to prevent the rifle dropping and to tie the position together. Once the sling has been attached it will be found even with moderate tension on the sling that the rifle, if pressed gently but sharply downward, will revert to its correct position.

Eye relief can be the same as for prone or slightly longer. Do not attempt to crane the neck forward or pull the head back but adopt a natural position. Most rearsights can be adjusted back and forth and a slightly longer eye relief is not a problem. Remember that if the eye relief is longer, a slightly larger rear aperture to obtain the same sight picture will be needed but only of the order of 0.1mm or so, or errors in the centring of the eye may occur.

To orientate the position horizontally, the whole postion should be turned as if on a turntable. For vertical errors the left hand should be moved backward on the forend to raise, and forward to lower, but remember

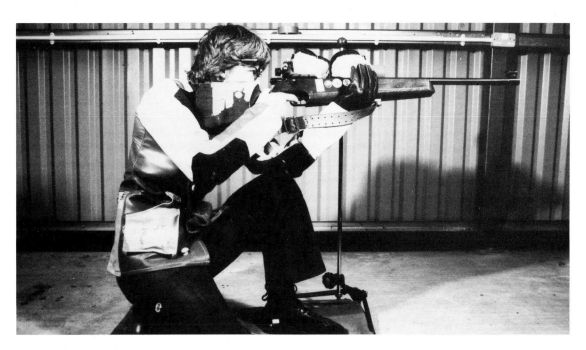

The shooter looks into the telescope with the left eye. A straight telescope is in use here; little movement is needed to look into it.

that only a small movement will make a large difference at the target, especially if a sloping forend, such as on a Standard Rifle is used. Move the handstop or sling swivel at the same time, obviously. Alternatives for vertical error are to move the left foot forward slightly or back, or to adjust the buttplate, but if this needs to be moved greatly then it would tend to indicate an incorrect position to start with, and with any major alteration it is advisable to look at the whole position.

Ensure that the head is correctly supported by the cheekpiece and that any adjustments needed to the woodwork, rather than available in the design of the rifle and its adjustments, should be undertaken carefully, and with due regard to the fact that the rifle will need to be used in other positions as well.

If the shooter has long legs it may be necessary to place the left foot forward and the left shin will then no longer be vertical. The left boot will need the fastenings adjusted to allow for the angle of the lower leg and the left foot will be somewhat further to the right than in the more usually seen position. An alternative to this is to place the left hand well forward on the forend but if the shooter has long legs and long arms a combination of these positions may well be necessary. If the low position is adopted then the left foot will also usually be forward as the left knee will be in a relatively high position to the trunk unless the shooter has short legs and a long trunk, together with short arms. It can thus be seen that the various body conformations may need a variety of positions to obtain the best results for each individual.

Gennardi Lushikov kneeling where he uses little cant.

Barry Dagger kneeling, showing the shorter stock adjusted for his height. He may not be tall but he is a giant in shooting and one of the very best kneeling shooters.

Reloading, kneeling with butt in shoulder.

Reloading, kneeling with butt taken out of shoulder.

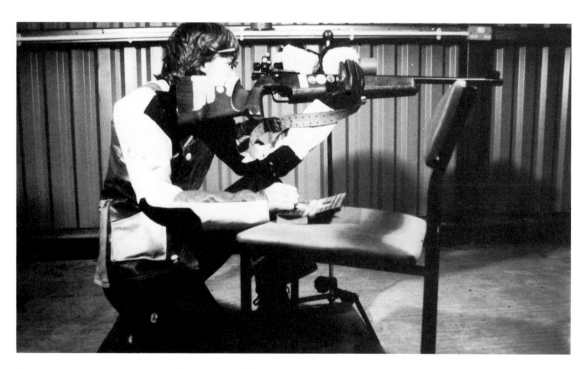

Using a chair or stool makes loading easy, and the shooter can reload in the shoulder if he wishes.

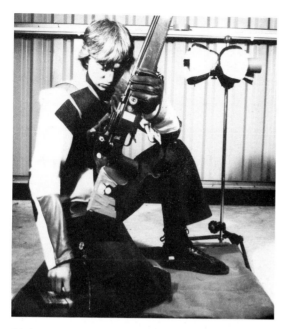

If there is no chair or stool, ammunition can be placed behind right leg and shooter should take the rifle out of the shoulder each time to prevent stretching.

Whereas the position as seen in the 1950s and early 1960s was fairly upright and relied mainly on balance, an overall tighter position has been adopted since then which relies less on balance. A more forward position of the body has also been seen although it should be emphasised that much of this apparent forward leaning is in fact the rolling of the shoulders, and the weight must still be carried by the support area. The upright and the forward leaning are certainly not two distinct positions although some shooters do tend to lean forward and there are variations in between to a greater or lesser degree.

Near perfect scores should be sought in the kneeling position and it is as steady as prone if possibly over shorter periods of time. Reloading may be done by keeping the butt in the shoulder or by dropping the butt, each time carefully replacing it in exactly the same position. Place the ammunition and target control on a stool or within easy reach just behind the right leg which will prevent any stretching to reach the ammunition and consequent upsetting of the position. Ensure that if the right leg starts to go numb you lean forward to relieve the weight and allow the blood a chance to circulate. Training will allow the shooter to stay in position longer without discomfort but may not entirely prevent the leg from starting to go numb. Some shooters stay in position for the whole forty shots and twenty is not usually a problem, but others take a break or lean forward.

6 Firing the Shot

CANT

Cant has been mentioned already but it is an important subject and should be considered separately as it is sometimes misunderstood.

Cant is the rotation or tilting of the rifle from the vertical. For the right-handed shooter this will be anti-clockwise or toward the head. Why is it necessary to cant? Simply to make the rifle fit the shooter or more precisely to enable the shooter to achieve an upright head position or as near an upright head position as possible. This is particularly important as any tilting of the head will induce sway as the vestibular organs – the organs of balance – will tell the brain that there is an imbalance and that it should be corrected. This is an over simplification but sufficient for our purpose. Also it is much better to have the eyes looking straight ahead out of their sockets rather than looking across the bridge of the nose or from under the eyebrows.

If it is possible to achieve an upright head and an upright rifle then cant will not be necessary, but this is not usually possible. A shooter should not be afraid to cant as it is no more difficult to achieve a constant angle of cant than it is any easier to keep a rifle always upright. Often it is found with a canted rifle that a better, more natural position can be obtained for the left hand and the pistol grip may also present itself at a better angle for the right hand.

What happens if the angle of cant or the rifle varies from upright? Consider an angle of six degrees, which is easy to imagine as it represents one minute on a clock face. At 100yds, for example, the group will be displaced 0.1in lower and 1.83in laterally, to the left with a right-handed shooter canting

his rifle to the left and with nil windage. Although the vertical difference is not great the lateral displacement is considerable. This occurs because the rearsight has to be elevated to allow for the drop of the bullet so that the group can be centred at the appropriate range. When the rifle is canted some of that elevation is lost and becomes windage and the group is displaced. It can therefore be seen that it is very important either to keep the angle constant or always upright.

At other ranges the effect is much the same although as the amount of elevation required to allow for the bullet's drop is different, so is the circle described by the canted rifle. It is an interesting experiment to shoot three shot groups at differing angles of cant at each range to see for yourself

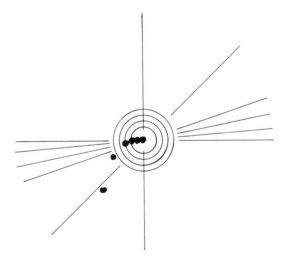

Cant. Copy of an actual target shot at 25yds with varying angles of cant. It shows that at the shorter ranges variation in angles of cant will have the same effect on scores as at the longer ranges.

Some shooters cant more than others. Gennardi Lushikov of the Soviet Union, a very fine shooter, cants a trifle more than most!

exactly what happens. If the rifle were to be completely rotated a circle would be described by the groups so fired.

The alternatives to cant do not always present a complete solution to keeping the head upright. Offset sights help but move the rifle from the centre of the position and the offset normally seen is about 1 cm. Cast off in the stock is usually built into most factory rifles and together with adjustments available in the buttplate go some way towards helping but most shooters find that they need more cast off than is available and a special stock would be expensive. Cant is therefore chosen by most shooters as the simplest method.

It is possible to control the angle of cant or the upright rifle by means of a spirit level mounted in the frontsight or attached to it or to one of the telescope blocks, but, although

this gives precise control, it is not permitted under Standard Rifle rules, so other methods have to be found. One way is to file the lugs on the frontsight insert so that it appears level, or with a transparent insert using a metal insert with the centre removed and the remaining bars used as levelling bars. If a post sight is used then the insert must be rotated, otherwise an unacceptable sight picture is presented, whereas some shooters rely on feel with the aperture frontsights. Some factory frontsights have an adjustable device so that levelling bars can be rotated to the appropriate angle, or an adjustable aperture or post attachment can be used most of which can be rotated before locking into position.

It has even been suggested that the angle of cant should be varied as a means of alteration for wind but this is not rec-

Gennardi Lushikov from the left side.

ommended as the various pressures on the rifle from the hands, head etc., may vary and change the position of the group from the alteration intended. The angles needed to obtain the adjustment needed in windage are too small to judge accurately and as you have paid good money for an adjustable rearsight why not use it. If the wind is changing quickly it is better to aim off than to try to alter the angle of cant.

One discipline in which cant is not recommended is that of the NRA Target Rifle which is shot at ranges from 300yds to 1,000yds. If cant were employed it would mean a changeable windage zero and that could be difficult. Better to suffer a poorer head position in this instance as the target is relatively large and such a precise hold is not so important, but precise control of the windage is necessary owing to the limited number of sighters allowed.

AIMING

It is necessary for the shooter to know which eye is dominant. This can be found with the parallax test by holding up a finger at arm's length, eyes open, pointing at an object and by closing first one eye then the other to determine which eye is the master, by observing with which eye the finger remains on the object. When viewing with the non-master eye the finger will be clearly to one side. An alternative method is to face squarely to another person who should be at some distance and point your finger at their right eye. The other person can then very clearly see to which eye the outstretched finger aligns. The shooter should always shoot with the master eye even if this means shooting left-handed when otherwise right-handed. The exception is if one eye has suffered injury when offset sights may be used instead. Although good results may be obtained by a shooter shooting right-handed with a left master eye it may be that full potential will not be realised. If a shooter is cross-dominant, that is right-handed with a left master eye or the reverse, always shoot from the master eye.

It is not necessary to have 20/20 vision, but it is important to achieve as near as possible to 20/20 vision by means of corrective lenses. These should be in spectacles and not in the rearsight. The spectacles move with the head so that if eye relief varies in different positions there is no problem; similarly if the rifle is held at differing angles of cant there is not the problem of adjusting the lens in the rearsight holder. Additionally, under UIT rules, a lens in the rearsight is not permitted, but naturally shooting glasses or spectacles are. Do ensure that when your eyes are tested the optician knows exactly what he is trying to achieve for you.

It is far better to keep both eyes open when shooting as the eyes work together and if one is covered or in darkness the other eye will dilate. Shooting with both eyes open is less fatiguing and for most people it is not difficult after a while, and means suppressing the visual image of the non-aiming eye. However, if after considerable trials this is still not possible then try a translucent shield a little distance from the non-aiming eye, which will still let in as much light as possible but prevents the non-aiming eye from being aware of the image.

Do give the eyes the best chance to work efficiently and keep the head as upright as possible with the eyes looking straight forward as nature intended, not across the bridge of the nose or from under the eyebrows. Distortion by aiming in an unnatural

A translucent blinder for the left eye may be used if shooting with both eyes open is otherwise impossible.

manner can induce problems for the eye which would not normally be there if looking straight out of the sockets.

Even at the very best it may be necessary to look at a slight angle, so if shooting glasses are worn ensure that the lens is at the correct angle, perpendicular to the line of sight and also that you are looking through the optical centre of the lens.

Ideal eye relief from the rearsight aperture is 40 to 45mm. However, this is not critical and may be up to 150mm. Often the rearsight will need to be moved from one position to another to keep the ideal eye relief but it may be found that the rearsight has insufficient movement rearward to achieve this distance. However, although not ideal it should still be within the larger distance mentioned.

The closer the rearsight aperture is placed to the eye, the larger it will appear and conversely the further away it is, the smalller it will appear. It is therefore desirable that some form of adjustable rearsight aperture is used. This will enable the shooter to select the same apparent size of aperture regardless of eye relief. Most shooters tend to use an aperture of 1.1mm, a few slightly smaller and a few more than this a little larger. Sizes still range from a minimum of 1.0 to 1.2mm with the optimum eye relief, but can range as large as 1.5mm with much longer eye relief. However, with an increased size it becomes less easy to centre the eye in the rear aperture. If an aperture is held up to a clear sky it is possible to see a dark centre to the aperture and it is through this dark centre that the shooter must aim. It will be found that with a reasonable-sized aperture the eye will find the centre without any particular effort and concentration can then be placed initially on getting the frontsight aperture in the centre of the rearsight, or the top in the centre of the aperture if a post or blade is used; and secondly and most importantly on the accurate alignment of the aiming mark in the centre of the frontsight aperture or correctly on top of the post, in

the latter case either tangent to the aiming mark or with a consistent line of white beneath the aiming mark.

It is most important that the focus is on the frontsight, not the aiming mark. Young shooters often let their focus shift back and forth from the frontsight to the aiming mark. This causes eye fatigue and is unnecessary as it is more important that the frontsight is clearly in focus at the expense of the aiming mark, rather than the reverse. If the frontsight is blurred the angular error is far greater than if the edges of the aiming mark are indistinct, and although many shooters feel that they can see both equally clearly this is not really possible. Shooters with poor sight or corrected vision must favour the frontsight and the aiming mark is often less distinct than they would like but results can be very good indeed.

The size of frontsight will vary depending on conditions. With the post or blade the width should be the same as the apparent width of the aiming mark, but it may be difficult to use this type of sight on multi aiming mark targets owing to the proximity of the other aiming marks. Certainly for standing it has its attractions as it has one point of aim and picks up movement more quickly, but although in past years the majority of international shooters used it standing and many used it for other positions also, its popularity has waned. However, do not dismiss it out of hand as some shooters are achieving very fine results with this style of frontsight.

The aperture is now used by the majority and may be either a metal insert or a plastic or glass aperture. The latter continues to gain in popularity with a pink-tinted insert proving to be the best colour. The metal insert should have a thin ring and the transparent insert a clear countersink or counterbore to the aperture or the aperture outlined in black. The size of the aperture depends on the illumination or visibility and the size of the target card. Some targets are printed on too small a size of card or with

A comfortable sight picture for a stable position

With a thin ring the amount of white looks greater and could be reduced slightly but it is fine as it is

A comfortable size for a good hold standing

The front sight aperture is too small

With a thin ring the amount of white may look acceptable but it is still too small

Line of white clearly visible

Once it touches the aiming mark where is it?

No. The post must be upright.

(Left)   Metallic inserts. (Right)   Transparent inserts with thin rings.

aiming marks so close together or near the edge that it artificially restricts the usable size of aperture. In very good illumination outdoors prone it is possible to use an aperture of say 3.4mm whereas in bright illumination it may be necessary to increase this to 3.6mm and with very bright illumination or in poor light conditions to increase to 3.8mm. This is prone where the hold is good and the movement is small. Unless the hold is good in the other positions it will be necessary to increase the sizes, and it is important that where the hold is not yet a good one that an aperture is chosen of such a size that the aiming mark does not 'bounce' against the inside of the aperture, otherwise it will have a tendency to make the shooter tense and so make conditions worse. For the air rifle it is necessary to use a larger aperture as the aiming mark is relatively larger and indoor lighting seldom as good as that outdoors. For all disciplines a thin ring does allow a slightly smaller aperture to be used than when using a thicker ring but do not overdo it.

One should take care that the metal insert is kept nice and black without any shiny parts, and in the case of the transparent insert that it is kept free from scratches and clear of dust as this will play havoc with the sight picture. If it does become scratched replace it and always handle with care. A small piece of tape or a cover should be fitted over the slot when using transparent inserts to keep out the light from the edge which would otherwise spoil the sight picture. Some frontsights have these as part of the design.

The rearsights on most rifles have adjustments per click of the windage and elevation knobs ranging from ¼ minute to ⅛ minute. A few have finer still, but the majority have 1/6 minute click adjustments. This is certainly fine enough. A minute of angle subtends about 26.59mm (1.047in) at 100 yds, half this at 50yds, and naturally somewhat more at 50m, with half again at 25yds. So with 1/6 minute clicks, this moves the group 1/6in at 100yds each click, 1/12in at 50yds and 1/24in at 25yds. Who needs anything finer? The manufacturers' booklets may tell you that one click moves the

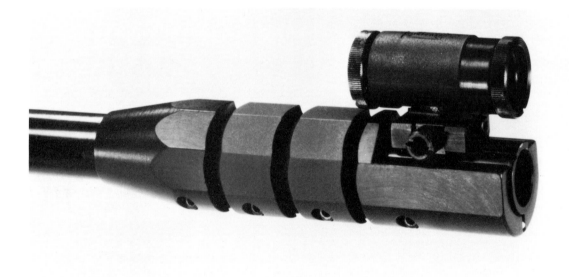

A frontsight mounted on an air rifle fitted with concentric adjustable barrel weights.

The Anschütz frontsight which may be adjusted for cant so that the levelling bars appear horizontal. There is also a cover fitted to keep out unwanted light from the slot into which inserts are placed.

point of impact 2. 5mm at 50m and this may well be so but try your sight for yourself by moving a large number of clicks, say forty up, forty right, forty down, and then forty left and see for yourself what the rearsight does. Shoot a group of three shots at each movement – this of course applies to any rearsight whatever the adjustment. Do not however talk in clicks but when speaking of adjustments talk in minutes. Not every-one's sights have the same value clicks and the individual shooter will know what the adjustment is if you talk in minutes regardless of how many clicks to the minute he or she may have on their rearsight.

Most rearsights move in a logical fashion; clockwise on the windage screw moves the sight to the left just as if you were using a screwdriver on a screw, similarly clockwise will move the sight down on the elevation screw. However, some British sights work in the opposite direction and no doubt you will come across sights with a combination of windage and elevation adjustments in different directions and some with unusual positioning of the adjustment knobs.

Make sure that your rearsight does not have too much backlash, in other words lost movement in the sight – the adjustment knob is turned but the sight does not move straight away. Some backlash is almost unavoidable but it should be attended to if the sight does not reverse direction in under

A typical rearsight which has numbered adjustment knobs, a light shade to the front and a rubber eye cup which may be cut to length.

one click. If you have to use such a rearsight, always move the sight in the same direction, i.e. if moving to the right half a minute or three clicks, move that amount, but if moving to the left half a minute or three clicks and you are aware that there is backlash present, move more than that backlash plus the adjustment then back again. This could mean moving to the left five clicks and back two to the right, ending up always moving the sight the same way.

It was because sights in past years were not so accurate in their adjustments that tube sights were popular. The tube sight consisted of a tube, usually baffled inside to prevent light reflections, mounted on a pair of telescope mounts. These are spring-loaded and were more positive in their adjustment than many of the conventional rearsights at that time. However, although some shooters still like tube sights for the

prone position they do restrict vision and are less favoured than formally. A later variant was a tube mounted at the front on a telescope-style mount but attached to a conventional rearsight, which found favour for some time but was rather a half-way house, although it did bring the adjustments nearer to hand, as did the shorter tube sights. The small tubes which screw into the front of the rearsight do a good job of cutting down unwanted light but are nothing akin to a true tube sight.

The majority of factory rifles are supplied with a single hole rearsight aperture which can be interchanged by unscrewing and replacing with another. This is adequate but not always convenient and many variations on the adjustable aperture are available, most of them working like a camera iris. Some are available with coloured filters which may be rotated at will, whilst others have a polarising filter, either two in the rearsight or one in the rearsight with the other element being in the frontsight. The coloured filters are very useful in various and varying light conditions but take care if change is made with a filter or an adjustable aperture during the shoot as it may change the point of impact. Try beforehand to see whether it is altered or not and then you will know whether you can change after sighters or not. Whether a rubber eye cup is used or not is down to personal preference; it does in some circumstances cut out unwanted light.

It is also possible to obtain adjustable frontsight apertures, either in metal form or with transparent apertures with adjustable centres. Some have the facility to change both the inside and the outside of the frontsight aperture within limits. Again these are very convenient but do not always give as thin a ring as desired and must, as with the rearsight aperture, be checked for concentricity.

A further variant of frontsight enables the aperture or levelling bars to be adjusted for cant, a very useful feature, although not entirely replacing the spirit level when it is permitted. Certainly without the adjustable feature being built into the frontsight tunnel itself it is necessary either to rotate the insert by filing the lugs, which is essential with a post frontsight, or get used to the angle at which the insert leans.

The spirit level may be placed either within the frontsight tunnel or externally or be mounted quite separately, either on a telescope block along the barrel or on the receiver. Remember that it is not permitted under the UIT rules when using the Standard Rifle, either in the women's events or at 300m in the Standard Rifle men's event.

The Diopter Optik

The diopter is an adjustable rearsight aperture like a camera iris, and should not be confused with the diopter optik which has a series of lenses which give a small magnifi-

cation and can be focused like a telescope. These were used for many years in Germany by the older shooters and enabled many to carry on shooting despite deteriorating eyesight. For some years a few countries have allowed them in metallic sight competitions by shooters regardless of age, but they are not permitted under UIT rules.

There are a number of patterns available, some with iris adjustable apertures and others with multi-hole apertures. Some may have coloured filters and/or polarising elements whilst others are without these additional features. However, they all have an adjustable feature which allows the frontsight to be brought into focus. This is advantageous for those shooters who have problems focusing on the frontsight but some find it disturbing that although the frontsight is clear, the target is less distinct than they would like. However, the latter is less important than keeping a clear frontsight, and when adjusting one of these devices it should have the aperture opened a shade more than one would normally use, then adjust the focus until the frontsight is clear at the expense of the target. If this is found to be too disturbing then at least favour the focus of the frontsight over the target. When this has been done, close down the rear aperture until it is slightly less than one would normally use with conventional sights. This will give a better picture and also help to keep the eye centred in the rearsight aperture. This is important as otherwise results will be poor with the eye out of centre.

Although they may not take the place of a good pair of shooting spectacles with correct lenses they do enable older shooters to continue to shoot with metallic sights and still achieve good results but care is required to get the best out of these diopter optiks.

Shooting Spectacles

Shooting spectacles are made so that when the shooter is in the correct shooting position the lens is correctly positioned so that the shooter looks through the optical centre of the lens and the lens is kept just away from the head to prevent perspiration from getting into it. The majority of shooting spectacles therefore have the aiming eye lens angled and they may either be adjustable or fixed permanently in the correct position. They may have one lens or two depending on whether the shooter feels more comfortable with a lens for the non-aiming eye. They can also be fitted with interchangeable filters or lenses. The lens should be prescribed by an optician who either knows the shooting sport or who has had explained exactly what is trying to be achieved. Most likely it will be necessary to take along your rifle in order that the spectacles can be fitted so that you look through the centre of the lens, remembering that this may vary for each position. If it does vary very much you may be better off with the adjustable pattern although many will find the variation small enough not to need any adjustment. Do be considerate and ask your optician if it is permitted to bring along your rifle before turning up with it!

The Telescope Sight

Although virtually unknown for target shooting in many countries and not permitted under UIT rules for three positional or prone shooting the telescope sight is very popular in the USA where half the National Championships are shot with it, in the so-called 'Any Sights' events. It is also popular to a lesser extent in some other English-speaking countries but for all shooters it is a very good training aid.

Modern telescope sights are either of the long pattern which mount on scope blocks on the barrel or else the short pattern which mount on the rifle receiver. Either pattern may have externally adjustable spring-loaded mounts or else have the adjustments internally and fixed mounts onto the rifle. The majority of recent telescopes have the

latter where the telescope itself does not move and this in itself is an advantage when moving from one range distance to another as it keeps a constant height of cheekpiece. However, the externally adjustable mounts are still very popular with shooters. The short pattern is naturally lighter but a few rifles cannot accommodate this pattern and have to use the longer style with the blocks on the barrel.

Various magnifications are manufactured and those suitable for small-bore target shooting can be anything from $15 \times$ to $36 \times$, with around $20 \times$ to $24 \times$ being the most popular. Even with the lower magnifications, when a shooter uses the telescope for the first time he may well be surprised at the amount of movement and pulse beat he sees. It is no different from normal but now that it is magnified and the target is clear the shooter can see it and take advantage of what he sees to reduce it and learn the hold pattern, and the optimum time at which to release the shot.

It is important to adjust the telescope correctly to achieve the best results. First look into the telescope at a clear blue sky and adjust the focus of the cross hairs or dot, whichever is the reticle; do not stare but look away until when you look into the telescope the cross hairs are sharp and clear. Then rest the telescope and adjust the object lens until the target is sharp and clear and when the eye is moved up and down and side to side the cross hairs do not move in relation to the target. This is very important, they should look as if they are pasted onto the target and must be in the same plane so that there is no chance of parallax being present. Otherwise when you use the telescope and move the eye out of the centre, if there is any parallax the group will also shift. Make a note of your settings as it is necessary to do this for each range at which you will use it; you will then be able to return to these settings knowing that parallax has been eliminated.

It is possible to rotate the internally adjustable telescope in the mounts so when

Prone from the right side whilst using a telescope sight.

the rifle is canted it is still possible to have the cross hairs upright. However, the externally adjustable spring-loaded mounts have location by means of a rib on the telescope and therefore the telescope cannot be rotated in the mounts.

On a good day if you have a good position and hold prone you should be able to keep the cross hairs well within the X ring, indeed some shooters claim that they can hold on to a bullet hole at 100yds which is only about ¼ minute of angle. On a bad day you may well find considerably more movement, but it is important to let the shot away at the same point in the hold pattern each time. You can learn a great deal with the telescope and although not an essential piece of equipment for most shooters it should certainly be considered by anyone who may have a little spare cash.

TRIGGERS AND TRIGGER CONTROL

Trigger mechanisms may be divided into four basic types:

Single stage: this pattern has no initial movement or take up prior to release which occurs when sufficient weight is applied to overcome the resistance when the rifle will fire.

Two stage: this pattern has an initial movement or take up before resistance of the second heavier stage is felt which will then release when sufficient weight is applied to overcome this resistance.

Set trigger: this mechanism is separate from the normal sear which holds back the cocked firing pin and is thus divorced from the weight of the firing pin spring. It has to be

97

cocked or set before use by a separate lever, often in the form of a second trigger, and when the firing or normal trigger is pulled releases a kicker which knocks the sear from the path of the firing pin. The trigger may be either single or two stage.

Electric trigger: this is a simple microswitch which, when sufficient pressure is applied, is activated and operates a solenoid to withdraw the sear from the path of the firing pin.

What are the advantages and disadvantages of each? The single-stage trigger has to have a shallow engagement if it is not to suffer creep or drag and then, if set at a reasonably light pull weight, care has to be taken when closing the bolt that this shallow engagement is not overridden and the rifle either does not cock or fires on closing of the bolt. It is not often seen when a light trigger weight is desired although it works adequately with trigger weights of 1.5kg or thereabouts. Another disadvantage is that there is no preliminary movement for the finger to get the feel of the trigger before the final stage, although it does mean that the finger can be accurately positioned for the one and only stage.

The two-stage trigger has in most mechanisms a deep engagement, most of which is removed as the first stage is taken up leaving a small amount to be overcome by the second stage. Therefore it should be safer than the single-stage trigger although there are a few manufactured that are really single-stage triggers mechanically as only the finger piece moves on the first pressure and not as part of the engagement. The initial stage allows the finger to make good contact with the trigger without fear of firing, but it is necessary to ensure that the finger is in the correct position when the second stage is pulled; this may mean that the position of the finger during the first stage may appear to be incorrect, until the trigger is pulled back to the second stage.

The set trigger has the disadvantage that it has a slower lock time than other patterns,

which means that it takes longer for the trigger to release the firing pin even if the time taken for the firing pin to strike the primer remains the same. This is owing to the separate mechanism with the kicker taking some time between its release and knocking out the sear from the firing pin. However, it does allow a very good feel to the trigger as it is divorced from the weight of the firing pin, and it is still popular on 300m rifles where the slower lock time is partly made-up by the shorter barrel time of the 300m cartridge compared to the small-bore. There are also some small-bore rifles made with a set trigger, often the companions of the 300m rifle and these are certainly very good. Some rifles have a self-setting trigger which is activated within the action and not by a separate lever or trigger in or around the trigger guard.

The electric trigger is very simple in that a microswitch takes the place of the trigger mechanism and when operated passes the current from a small battery in the stock to a solenoid which withdraws the sear. It is designed to give warning of the battery failing often by simply not functioning and are now mainly reliable; however, they are not necessarily quicker in lock time than the conventional mechanical trigger. They do have one advantage in that they can be placed anywhere which can be a boon for anyone developing a rifle for a handicapped shooter who may have to operate the trigger with the same hand supporting the forend.

Trigger Weight

It is not at all desirable to have a trigger that is very light. A trigger pull weight of less than 200g gives no real advantage, but many shooters do use weights of 150 to 170g with success. Many uninformed shooters using as light a trigger as possible in the standing position who believe that they will be able to get the shot off when the hold is good would actually be better off using a heavier weight standing of 200g plus so that there is no temptation to get the shot off quickly and usually poorly. For most shooters the standing position is not steady enough to use a light trigger even if they are able to get away with it in the steadier prone and kneeling positions.

In the case of a two-stage trigger, the first stage should have about two-thirds of the weight in the case of a trigger with a fairly heavy pull weight and the final stage the additional one-third. This not only allows a positive variation and hesitation between the two stages but makes the second stage feel lighter than it really is as two-thirds of the pull weight is already taken up by the finger. With a light trigger this would leave insufficient feel of the second stage and the first stage must be proportionately lighter, so that the second stage is quite definite.

The trigger weight should increase both before and after release and there should neither be a sudden collapse nor a sudden stop after release. If a trigger stop is fitted it should be backed off sufficiently that the trigger does not hit it after release, disturbing the aim.

The finger must pull the trigger directly to the rear without any pressure to the side and the position of the finger on the trigger must be exactly the same for each and every shot, thus there must be no variation in placement up or down the finger piece nor must the finger be pushed further through the trigger guard for one shot than another. The finger must be free to move and clear of the rifle stock. If it is not, remove the small amount of wood necessary to provide this clearance. The part of the finger which rests on the trigger is from the first pad to the first joint but not beyond. The first pad is favoured by many shooters for the lighter triggers with the first joint for those with a heavier pull. However, this is not inviolable and many shooters use the first pad for all triggers whilst others use the first joint all the time.

For beginners, pulling the trigger is a conscious and deliberate action with concentration moving back and forth from the hold

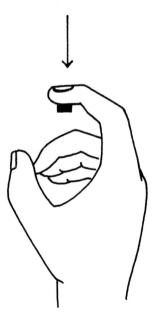 

First pad or up to first joint but not beyond, and pressure always directly to the rear.

to trigger control. For the more experienced shooter the trigger operation becomes subconscious and concentration can be devoted more to the evaluation of the hold and external conditions such as wind and mirage.

It should be noted that the word 'pull' not 'squeeze' has been used. Squeeze denotes pressure between two points or even contraction of the whole hand which is not what is required. If the shooter were to squeeze the trigger say between trigger finger and thumb, the trigger would release after the required pressure had been applied but it would not be possible to immediately stop the opposite pressure that the thumb had applied and there would be another variable creeping in. The only thing that should move is the trigger finger with the hand itself properly anchored. The right hand should grip the pistol grip with exactly the same pressure each time which has been described as the pressure needed to lift a wet milk bottle. The wrist should be straight to enable the trigger finger to operate in the best possible conditions.

Trigger shoes to widen narrow triggers can be useful but do not make them too wide and certainly to place a trigger shoe on some of the factory triggers is totally unnecessary resulting in an over wide trigger which will present the risk that some sideways pressure will inadvertently be applied.

Trigger Operation

The novice will have so much else to think about that the best way to operate the trigger is to increase the pressure on the trigger continually until it releases, unless the sight picture (the hold) becomes unacceptable. This can be denoted on a graph of weight and time as almost a straight line in the case of a single-stage trigger. With a two-stage trigger there will be a straight line until the first stage has been taken up, then a pause as this weight is held, and an almost straight line as the second stage is overcome.

As the shooter progresses and the hold becomes better the final amount of weight to be overcome may be taken in stages by an increase in pressure as the hold improves, holding this pressure if the hold deteriorates and applying further pressure as the hold improves again and so on until the trigger releases. This all happens quickly and as the shooter gains experience it becomes more and more a subconscious action, triggered off as the sight picture approaches perfection. Remember that when the sight picture is perfect it is not necessarily the correct time to increase pressure on the trigger as by the time the brain has evaluated the sight picture, passed the message to the finger and the rifle mechanism has operated and sped the bullet on its way, the best time may well have passed. Only if the position is very stable and a very good hold maintained can the trigger be pulled when the sight picture is perfect. It is a matter of knowing the hold pattern and increasing pressure just as the most perfect sight picture the shooter can achieve is approaching, not when it is already there because that may well be too late. It also tends to lead to 'snatching' or increasing the trigger pull too rapidly in an attempt to beat the deterioration of the sight picture which will only lead to a rather poor shot at best.

A few very good shooters use the impulse method of trigger control. This can be illustrated on the graph by a very rapid build-up in pressure in the last stages but it should be stressed that this is well controlled and does not provide unwanted movement of the rifle. Many shooters use a combination of the graduated and impulse methods. A further method to be seen is the one in which the trigger finger is continually moving, taking up and releasing some pressure and finally taking up more pressure and overcoming the final resistance. This takes a great deal of training to be effective although some very good shooters do use it.

For the beginner who may find trigger control less than easy it is a good idea to have

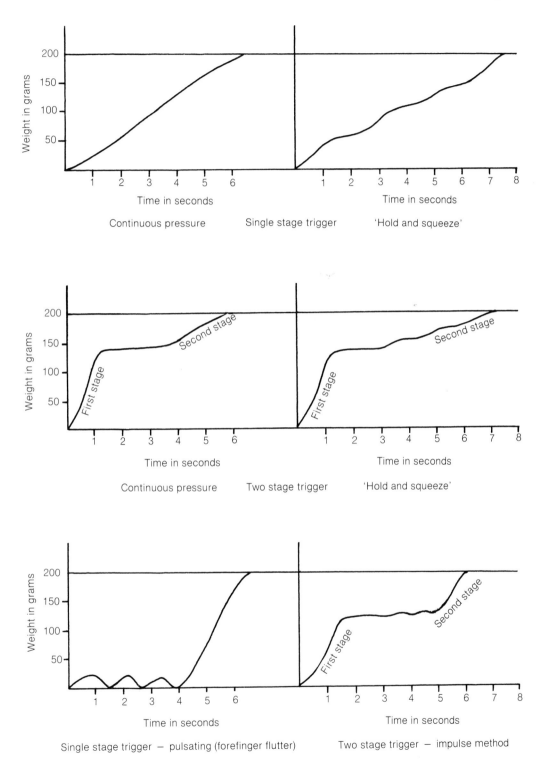

Trigger control.

an experienced hand over the pupil's to show exactly what is required. Finally, the all important act of follow through cannot be overstressed. Follow through until the bullet has passed clear through the target and do not become interested in anything else until that act has been completed. The beginner is particularly anxious to see what result has been achieved but instil in him or her from the very beginning that the result will be so much better if the follow through is good and the reward when the shot is spotted in the telescope will be that much greater.

FOLLOW THROUGH

What is follow through? You will hear this term in many sports and it has the same meaning in all. In rifle shooting it is the art of continuing the actions and control required to fire a shot until after that shot has passed clear through the target.

If there is no follow through, the subsequent shot may be poor as the control needed to effect a good trigger release may well have broken down before the trigger has released the sear. The sight picture may well have long gone before the bullet is only part way down the barrel, the hold may well have disintegrated before the firing pin has struck the primer, the recoil will not be absorbed exactly the same each time and, of course, maximum repeatability is the name of the game. It is therefore vitally necessary to stimulate all the actions required to produce the perfect shot so that each of these actions continues well after the actual time required of them. Just as a golfer does not stop the swing as soon as the ball is hit or a boxer his fist at the point of contact, so must the shooter follow through.

The hold must be maintained, the sight picture must remain, the breath must still be held, the arousal level must be maintained at the correct level and the trigger control continued well after the sear has been released so that, as has already been said but

should be repeated, the bullet has passed clear through the target.

It may sound simple, but in a match follow through is the first thing to suffer. It is easy to observe when watching a shooter that this has happened. Anxiety is the usual cause, over the shot being good or bad, over wishing to look into the telescope to determine the value or position of the shot, over whether the wind or mirage judgement was correct and over loss of face or loss of self-esteem.

If the shooter, even though possibly suffering from anxiety, or a bad hold could follow through just a little longer than usual, he may well find that what appeared to be a not so good shot, will turn out better than anticipated (and anticipate is the word because that is what so many shooters do when follow through becomes short).

Lack of follow through or too short a follow through is often the cause of a good small-bore shooter finding that air rifle scores are comparatively poorer. The longer time taken for the pellet to exit the barrel needs a longer follow through and the same applies to a full-bore shooter who may find some difficulty obtaining equal results with the small-bore rifle.

The final act after follow through is to call the shot – to make a mental note of exactly where it is believed the shot will be from the information imparted as the shot is fired. Was the sight picture correct, was the trigger control perfect and did the rifle recoil exactly the same as it normally does? Each of these questions in combination with information from preceding shots can give information upon which to judge the following shot and whether any sight alteration is needed or some other correction.

BREATHING AND THE HEART CYCLE

During the aiming process and the actual firing of a shot the shooter must hold his breath for if he did not the resultant movement would create conditions that would make an accurate shot impossible. At rest the average person has approximately twelve to fifteen breaths per minute. Inhalation and exhalation lasts about two seconds, whilst there is a pause between each respiratory cycle of two seconds. This period would naturally be too short for the shooter to release the shot but it is possible to extend the pause for some twelve seconds without any ill effect.

If you try for yourself you will notice that it is possible to hold the breath longer on inhalation than exhalation, and that on inhalation there is more effort required and some tension, whilst on exhalation the muscles are more relaxed. However, tests have shown that there is less pulsation when holding the breath on inhalation than when holding the breath on exhalation, so this slight tension of the muscles is of some help.

Although it is possible to extend the breathing cycle pause by some twelve seconds this period is in excess of that required to complete aiming and fire the shot. Very few leading shooters take longer than six seconds to complete the action of firing a shot, including follow through and many take considerably less. It must indeed be remembered that the first effect to be felt is not the strain of wishing to breathe again but that the shooter's concentration will be diminishing. It is therefore desirable that the shot is fired within about six seconds.

Before the pause the shooter should be breathing normally, then take two or three deeper breaths before holding the breath in preparation to firing the shot. After the shot has been fired and follow through completed it has been found by tests that most of the leading shooters exhale before continuing the normal breathing cycle. Before the next shot the shooter should inhale more deeply than normal a few times, then breathe normally before the breathing cycle for the next shot. This may sound involved but it soon becomes routine and in reality takes very little time. However, take care that breathing does not become too deep or hyperventilation may occur.

Each shooter must see for himself how much breath must be held during the pause; this varies between holding just after the beginning of inhalation or up to a half-breath, but not more than this.

During the act of firing a shot and the breath cycle the heart continues to beat and this beat transmits movement to the rifle which is visible in the sight picture. Although it may not be very noticeable when using iron sights, it certainly is when using the telescope sight. When the shooter is under match pressure any movement seen is usually the heartbeat, often only magnified by the shooter's heightened awareness when what has always been there can be clearly seen. This heightened awareness is like putting on the telescope sight; it does not increase the movement but just shows the shooter that it exists. Obviously if the arousal level is too high and the shooter does

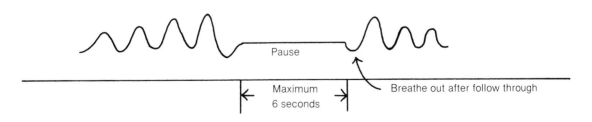

Pause

Maximum
6 seconds

Breathe out after follow through

Breathing cycle whilst shooting.

nothing to reduce this level then the movement could well be greater than normal and the heart rate increased.

Just as with breathing there is a pause between beats and the shooter should try to release the shot just before the next heart-beat. This may sound difficult but with training it becomes achievable and learning can be speeded up by putting the telescope on the rifle.

It is not desirable that the competitive shooter should have a heartbeat like that of a cross-country skier for example, which is very powerful. It is better to have a heartbeat which is quiet without a powerful thump that would be so disturbing to the shooter.

7 Cleaning

CLEANING

Much has been written on the pros and cons of cleaning the rifle barrel, but any precision instrument works more efficiently when clean. Certainly rifles differ in how many rounds may be fired before it is necessary to clean them before accuracy suffers, but then it should not be left so long that the shooter finds out that he is about to have to clean his rifle when it is too late. The very rare rifle will appear to shoot well even if the barrel is left well alone but this is the exception rather than the rule. Certainly barrel life can be extended if the barrel is cleaned regularly and no one wants to lose a good accurate barrel through the want of a few minutes spent on cleaning. Somewhere between 100 and 500 rounds is about right.

Cleaning should be undertaken with care and the implements used should themselves be protected and kept clean. There is no use in cleaning a barrel with a cleaning rod covered with dirty fluid and embedded with grit which combine to make a paste to wear the very barrel you are trying to protect. The best cleaning rod is made of highly polished steel which is less likely to pick up grit than a plastic-coated rod, but both are quite acceptable providing they are kept clean. To this end it is a good idea to keep them in a sealed aluminium tube which is a push fit onto the ferrule of the rod. Even this tube must be kept clean so wipe the rod thoroughly before putting it away. It is sad to see so many rods just thrown into the car after use without thought as to what they may pick up.

When cleaning a bolt-action rifle a rod guide must be used, not only to guide the rod into the barrel and protect the chamber from wear, but also to protect the action and particularly the trigger from cleaning solvent and fouling. Keep the cleaning rod guide clean and make sure that it does not have any sharp edges which may abrade the rod.

The style of jag used is a matter of personal preference, both the type on to which the patch is rolled and the button style are very popular. Another pattern uses a felt pad which is placed on to the end of the jag and fits the barrel tightly. Unless you are drying the barrel after cleaning or before use, the patch should not enter the barrel without solvent on it; do not put a dry patch down a dirty barrel. There are various solvents which do the job well, some of which attack the fouling from the top whilst others get under the fouling – but many of them contain substances which should not be brought into contact with the skin so wash your hands thoroughly after cleaning.

Two types of brush are required, a bronze bristle brush and a hog's bristle brush which goes under a variety of names. The bronze brush used with solvent does an efficient job of removing the fouling although some shooters worry that it might harm the barrel. Certainly many shooters use them judiciously without reporting any harm. The hog's bristle brush is made of strong hairs and must also be used with solvent.

When cleaning the rifle, insert the bolt guide, then pass a brush soaked in solvent through the barrel a couple of times; follow this with a well-soaked patch and if there is time, place the rifle muzzle down in a metal container, not plastic as the solvent may attack it. It will surprise you to see how much rubbish comes out of the barrel. Dry out thoroughly and if not using the rifle right

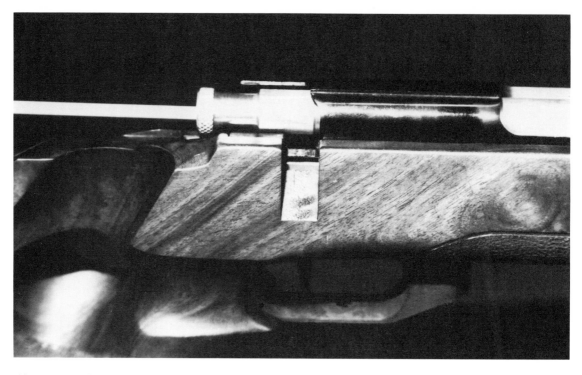

Always use a cleaning rod guide.

away leave a small amount of protective solvent or oil in the barrel to prevent corrosion.

At the same time clean the bolt face, extractors and firing pin and very lightly oil the latter if necessary. Clean around the end of the barrel both at the breech and the muzzle, the latter with particular care as any damage here can impair accuracy and could necessitate recrowning. Ensure that no fluid has entered the trigger mechanism, and if it is wet either from fluid or rain follow the manufacturer's instructions as to what lubrication to use and where it may be needed; if uncertain seek expert advice for the future. This may mean removing the rifle from the stock and when replacing ensuring that the bedding area is clean and dry, replacing the barrel and action carefully, making sure that it is seated back against the recoil shoulder or that the recoil shoulder on the action is seating correctly in the bedding. Tighten the stock bolts to the manufacturer's speci-

fications unless variation in the tension on the stock bolts has been found to be beneficial to accuracy, in which case return to the same settings.

The exterior of the metal parts should be very lightly oiled to protect from corrosion but special attention must be paid to the sights. A mixture of oil, dust and sand etc. from the range makes a very effective grinding paste, so take care that the sight threads and slides are kept very clean with only enough oil to enable them to function and you will be rewarded with much longer accurate service. If you have any filters or glass in the sights it is only common sense to remove these before cleaning as you do not want to have to take apart an iris filter combination unnecessarily. Take particular care of any transparent frontsight elements which do not take kindly to some solvents, and avoid scratches.

Look after the stock as you would a nice piece of furniture, because although one sees many a knocked about stock on a rifle which shoots very well, surely it is better to have a rifle which looks good as well as shoots well.

What about cleaning the air rifle and the CO_2 rifle as most of these cannot easily be cleaned from the breech? Hard felt pads can be obtained for cleaning the barrel and these are shot in the same way as a pellet but take care that they are aimed at a backstop in the same way as a pellet because they do exit at a high velocity. It usually requires two of these to clean the barrel although if it has been neglected a brush with some solvent on it can be drawn through from the breech on a rod inserted from the muzzle. Take care that the rod is centered as it is drawn through, as any wear at the muzzle can be just as detrimental to air rifle accuracy as to the small-bore rifle. Many air rifles have the actual muzzle a long way down the extension tube which carries the frontsight, so care has to be taken to find this muzzle. Cleaning rod guides are available for some makes that enable them to be more easily cleaned from the muzzle. Often shooters are seen to use a pull-through for the air rifle but this is not advisable with any rifle as damage at the muzzle can all too easily result. Protect the action from solvent running into it, whch may be less easy than with the small-bore rifle. Dry out the barrel after solvent has been used before shooting.

8 Competition Shooting

Although there are a few who do not enter competitions nearly everybody in the target shooting world is a competitive shooter. Having been a member of a club for a while and having shown a reasonably consistent even if a low score, entry is usually made for most shooters in some competition or other, often in a league team where shooters of a similar standard shoot against each other. No shooter needs to feel that he or she is not good enough to compete as competitions are available to cater for every standard. As the shooter becomes more proficient so progress is made through the various teams, or classes of the individual competitions.

It is an excellent idea to shoot in shoulder-to-shoulder matches as soon as possible, in fact the postal shooting which is so popular in some countries is virtually unknown in most. Whereas small-bore shooting is popular indoors during the winter, the newcomer should start shooting outdoors as soon as possible. Many countries do little if any small-bore shooting indoors leaving indoor shooting to the air rifle.

PREPARATION

It is important for any shooter, whether a beginner or advanced to prepare properly for the shoot. Do not arrive at the range at the last minute uncertain whether you have all your equipment and with no time to sort yourself out, as this is a recipe for a poor result. Make sure that you have a check-list for your equipment and tick off each item before you get it ready to take with you; make sure that it is all in good order and with nothing left out. Get to the range in good time so that you can relax after

carrying heavy equipment cases or bags. Know exactly what time you are shooting and arrive at least one hour before you have to fire your first shot. If the range is more than 150km away leave the night before if you have to shoot in the morning. Find out where the range is – most entry forms have a map or at least details of how to get there – but even then ranges are not always the easiest places to find.

It may sound obvious to take the right sort of clothing but shooters often turn up at a shoot where they have to walk down the range and change targets without good wet weather gear on the most awful days. Even at an indoor competition it can still be colder than you might wish. Make sure that you have something to eat and drink with you unless you are certain that refreshments are available. Do not drink coffee on the day of the match before your shoot as this will increase your movement visibly whether you are a habitual coffee drinker or not.

If you are travelling the evening before try to spare time to look at the range to see if there are any unusual features which could influence the wind such as gaps in the hedges or stop butts at different distances. On the day of the match be particularly observant as soon as you arrive for wind conditions, mirage etc. Even if a well-meaning friend offers to hang the target for you, walk down the range as well; you may see factors which could affect the wind or other unusual features which may be of assistance. Even for the relative beginner at least you can feel the wind for yourself down the range even if your experience so far does not let you consider further factors.

If conditions are really bad – high winds, rain, snow, cold or excessive heat – do not be put off. It may put some shooters off but you must be positive: as you cannot change the conditions make the most of them. There is far more satisfaction in coming away with the best score of which you are capable than to bemoan your fate and come off with a poor result which you know full well you could have improved upon if you had knuckled down to it despite the bad day. Going home, at least you can feel good about the result – it may not be wonderful but you can say that you have done your best. You really have two alternatives: make the best of it or make a mess of it.

SIGHTERS

Every full-bore shooter is aware how essential it is to know the zero of his rifle as the numbers of sighters are strictly limited or may not be permitted at all. Therefore not only is it necessary to know the windage zero but also the exact setting for each range. The windage zero is the position on the sights at which the shots in a nil wind condition would group in the centre of the target, and most sights are fitted with a scale that can be adjusted so that it is possible to return to this setting at any time, and on some sights the setting can be easily read so that it is possible to know exactly how much windage adjustment is in use at any time during the shoot. It is just as sensible to know one's zero in small-bore shooting, and zero targets are available for small-bore as well as full-bore. The zero target must be placed upright on the stopbutt, preferably using a plumb line to ensure that it is precise. The rifle can then be shot and a note made of the sight setting for use in a nil wind condition at each range, and at the same time a note made of the elevation setting. It can readily be seen how much alteration in the windage setting is needed when altering from one range to the next when the shooter cants, and this can mean a considerable saving in sighters and a more useful employment of the sighting

target. The sights which have a vernier scale are much easier to use than those without, but it is possible with any sights to keep a record of the settings.

The sighting shots can be the most important shots that you shoot during the match. This is particularly true outdoors as they are probing shots to find out exactly what the conditions are doing on a particular range whilst you are shooting. They are not shots to be fired as practice or to see if you can get tens and when you do to go on to the match card. If this is what you use the sighter for then the final result will not be as good as you could achieve if you used the sighter intelligently.

Most barrels do not put the first shot from a cold barrel into the same place as subsequent shots and therefore it is a good idea to fire one, two or more shots if necessary away from the centre of the sighter to avoid cluttering up the higher scoring rings. Do make sure that they are shot within the confines of the buttstop or pellet catcher. If shooting on the three card system where any shot below the line may count, make sure these are shot slightly high rather than low on the sighter.

Naturally you will have adjusted the sights for the range at which you are shooting and selected a suitable frontsight insert for the prevailing light conditions. If you are shooting indoors and you have come prepared for the match the sighters will be few in number and will confirm to you that all is well, that the frontsight is well chosen and the sight settings are correct. If this is not the case make the necessary adjustments and have one or two more sighters before starting the match card. The sighter is not for settling down; you should do this before you start the sighter, before you fire the first shot. Take time before you start and you may well finish first in more ways than one.

Shooting outdoors the sighter takes on a different role when it is used to confirm the conditions. Adjust your rearsight to what you feel is the best wind condition on which

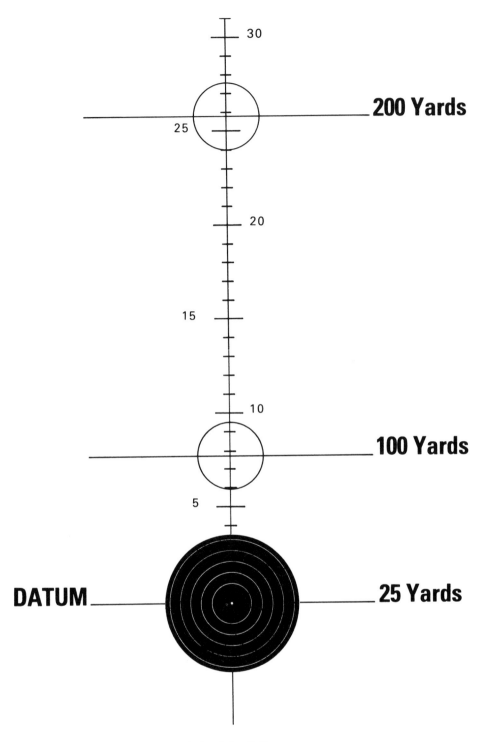

200 Yards

100 Yards

DATUM

25 Yards

A typical zeroing target. This target from the National Small-Bore Rifle Association of Greater Britain is designed for use at 25yds and incorporates distances up to 200yds, which is rarely used now. The graduations are in minutes of angle.

to shoot. This is done only after careful observation to see what is the most frequently occurring condition that is consistent in both strength and direction, and which gives you sufficient time in which to get off a good shot. Fire two shots on that chosen condition to confirm that your estimate has been correct, then fire a further two or three shots on a second wind condition which, although not as frequent or as consistent as the first, appears to be a second possibility if the first chosen condition disappears or does not remain for such long periods. Make a note as to where the shots go on this second condition so that it will be a simple matter to alter the sights with certainty if necessary. If the wind is blowing across the range fire a shot on its lowest and also its highest strength to see how far these shots will be taken. If it is a fishtailing wind switching from one side then the other, it will be necessary to fire a shot when the wind is blowing from one side then the other to see how far the bullet will be taken. Note also how much elevation change will be needed as the wind does not only blow the bullet horizontally but has a vertical element in it as well, the wind carrying the bullet from ten o'clock to four o'clock and the stronger the wind the more vertical element in it.

Only when you have this 'map' do you go on to the match card. Even if shooting on the three card system where it is possible to go back on to the sighter at any time it is sensible to follow this routine for the sighter. It will save a lot of valuable time and the sighter may become so cluttered with shots that you will not know which one is the shot just fired. With a telescope sight it is a slightly different matter as you can aim anywhere on the paper in the vicinity of the sighter and observe the fall of the shot which it is not possible to do with iron sights. Even so time is not unlimited, and whilst going back on to the sighter the wind can change and change back again when returning to the match card. Owing to refraction, aiming at a target at a different height may cause errors due to looking through air of different density at different levels from the ground, and the sight line in consequence will be bent. This can occur with either type of sight and if, after coming off the sighter, the shots are displaced vertically and perhaps again when moving down to the bottom targets it is most likely that refraction is present. You can do little about it but at least you are forewarned if you are aware of it. It might not be your position that you have failed to adjust from one target to the next but take care that you have done this before blaming refraction.

There is a method by which you can be forewarned of refraction in the horizontal plane. It is not visible with the eye but if a cross hair is placed in the spotting telescope and the telescope mounted on a rigid stand it is possible to see the target apparently move in relation to that cross hair indicating that refraction is in existence. However, as there may be parallax with this arrangement do not get confused. It is possible to see the target apparently move up and down as well as sideways and if this arrangement is used with some care it can avoid an otherwise lost point. If the stand is on a grass firing point make sure that it is firmly pressed into the ground or some settling movement may be misinterpreted. With some telescopes it is a fairly simple matter to fit this cross hair in an advantageous position whilst with others it is less simple. If you have a target telescope sight it is possible to obtain an adaptor so that it can be mounted on a spotting telescope stand which can then be used and with all parallax eliminated.

WIND AND MIRAGE

It is the conditions outdoors that make for so much more of a challenge than when shooting indoors. It is just as difficult to shoot in poor conditions at 100yds as it is at 1000yds and, indeed, often far more difficult. That little forty grain bullet is certainly affected by the wind even at the middle distances. Some wind on the range is the prevailing wind, some is the differential heating of the ground and air. Hot air rises and is replaced by cooler air which is then drawn in. The hot air does not just rise vertically but moves upwards in an anti-clockwise direction. Many rifle ranges are constructed with the firing point under cover or in a building and so cooler than the area between the building and the stop butt which also produces shade. The sides of the range are usually protected by walls, fences or banks which also produce shade. When the sun is shining the open area of the range is warmer than the surroundings which produces ideal conditions for a wind which rotates. Almost every shooter must have seen flags or other wind indicators pointing in different directions on the range but failed to observe that they are pointing in a general form of a circle. Ranges vary in width and length so do not expect to see a perfect circle and there may even be more than one. These revolving winds are only really visible when there is little prevailing wind which tends to cover them. On a wide range with many firing points these revolving winds are blown along by the prevailing wind and therefore a differing wind is presented to the shooter as they pass. Additionally the direction of refraction is opposite each side of their centre and this can be seen by a rigid telescope with cross hairs or the rifle telescope mounted in the same fashion. It can be seen therefore that even if all of one class of shooter is placed down together they do not necessarily all get equal conditions under which to shoot. When a cloud cools the range the wind may stop or with rapid cooling may start moving the other way around, and take care in the southern hemisphere as the reverse occurs both with heating and cooling.

What is the best wind indicator? For moderate winds up to twelve mph the answer is easy: mirage, providing there is enough of it to make use of it. Its advantages are that it is instantaneous where all other indicators are historical, it computes the plusses and minuses between the telescope in which it is observed and the place at which it is focused. This is normally short of the target so the important distance is covered. It also computes any changes of angle in the wind; this is because when the wind changes from say nine o'clock to eleven o'clock the distance the wind covers is the same but appears relatively shorter in the telescope because it is viewed from the same place whilst the wind is travelling at a different angle and the mirage appears to have slowed down, which in fact is the effect on the bullet from a wind change of that type. Imagine a vehicle travelling straight across in front of you and then imagine the same vehicle travelling at the same speed at an angle towards you. The distance travelled across the front of you is relatively less.

Mirage must always be viewed against a dark background, the edge of the target frame or target changer. With experience even small changes can be seen and the sights adjusted when necessary. The disadvantage of mirage is that above twelve mph it flattens out and becomes of little use and it is not visible in rain so that other indicators must be used. Also mirage can often be seen but not well enough to use whilst actually shooting. It can be seen with the mounted telescope that mirage also moves the target in the same direction in which it runs. Do not shoot when mirage boils, that is bubbles upwards, as this means that it is still or coming towards you or going away and the apparent position of the target will be changed vertically with consequent effect on the position of the shot.

Flags as wind indicators come a poor second – the UIT specify the material, the size and the placing of the flags which gives some uniformity, but many domestic range flags vary from good to bad each differing in its interpretation of the wind. Many flags also do not give a good indication of any change of angle and all are historic. Their inertia has to be overcome and it is always advisable to look at a flag up wind to get the earliest possible warning. Having said that, they can give good indication of wind changes and may well be all you have to go by. They tend to give a better indication if they are being lifted by the wind rather than when the wind is dropping off and the flags are going down, although it is also normally true that a rising wind is more consistent than a falling one.

Although the shooter has to observe the mirage in the telescope, then sight and let the shot off, the small delay if the telescope is well positioned will certainly be less than the historical aspect of the wind flag. With mirage the first thing to do after follow through is to look into the telescope again to confirm the mirage, before looking for the position of the shot. If relying on flags, after follow through observe the flag for any change.

There are many other indicators of wind such as dust, smoke from rifles, noise, trees, bushes, grass, the fall of shot, the fall of other people's shot although care should be taken here as they may be aiming off or not be very good shooters or wind dopers.

The important thing is to try to get the shot off in the same wind conditions each time, that is the importance of the sighter; you also have a second condition as a back up. Do take care that the shot release and the follow through do not suffer. If you get the wind right and muff the shot that will not help and the old saying that 'a good hold is worth two minutes of wind' remains true although with today's targets two minutes is rather large.

It is to be remembered whatever wind indicator is used that the important area is that nearest to the shooter. If the bullet is deflected at the start it will continue to be deflected at that angle to the target whereas if the wind influence is nearer the target it may be deflected the same amount, but the angle will be over a shorter distance and

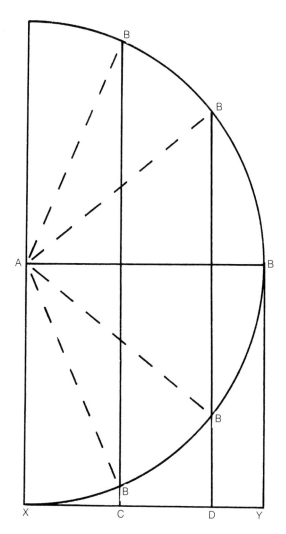

Mirage. When wind changes angle but not velocity it travels over the same distance A – B during the same time, but when observed in the telescope from the firing point X – Y it appears to slow the nearer it approaches, blowing directly at or away from the observer. This is because the distances over which it is observed to travel across the range X – C, X – D for example are shorter, therefore mirage by slowing or speeding up can indicate not only a change in wind velocity but a change in wind angle. When the wind blows directly toward or away from the shooter the mirage boils.

therefore the effect at the target less. Remember the important part to watch is that area nearest you; but do be aware that the range building may influence the wind pattern nearer to you particularly if the wind is coming from behind. The first part of the range may then be in an area with very little wind so you must take into account the activity further down range. You must also do this if there are significant gaps in the banking or hedges around the range.

It has already been mentioned on page 51 that windage is seldom needed at exactly nine or three o'clock and this is because of the effect of the wind on the rotating bullet. Rifling twists are generally clockwise or to the right and it is unlikely that you will come across a rifling twist to the left in a small-bore target rifle. The effect is that when a wind increases from the left the bullet will be deflected toward four o'clock and when the wind increases from the right it will be deflected toward ten o'clock. Similarly, if the wind backs off or decreases after blowing from the left, the shot, if the group has been fired allowing for the wind, will also go toward ten o'clock. Naturally, if the wind decreases after blowing from the right and the group had been central, the shots will fall toward four o'clock.

It is not necessary to go into the reasons why this should occur and it is not entirely caused by one effect; it has been well detailed by various scientists, though some tend to give contra-indications if studied alone. Those interested should look up Daniel Bernoulli (1700–1782) whose Bernoulli theorem is well known, together with the Magnus effect and Sperry's law.

The stronger the wind the greater the vertical element in the deviation of the bullet, and it is no surprise that in some of the strong winds shooters encounter on exposed ranges, many shots are lost for elevation as well as for the expected windage at 100yds. It is plain to see when looking at targets shot under conditions of varying wind that there is a strong ten to four o'clock spreading of this group.

It can therefore be seen that even if the rifle is held upright, elevation adjustment will be needed as well as windage in conditions of vary-

ing wind; and that with a right-handed shooter canting the rifle more elevation adjustment will be needed, whilst the left-handed shooter may well find that the angle of cant matches the angle at which the wind blows the bullet under most commonly experienced shooting conditions.

If you have the ability to shoot quickly, particularly in a wind, there will be fewer wind changes and you can take advantage of any consistent wind and get some shots into the ten ring before it changes. Some shooters are naturally slow shooters and it is a mistake for them to try to shoot quickly, although they may be able to smooth their technique and reload quickly so as not to waste any valuable time. Do not waste time peering into your telescope at a shot that may be hanging on as it will not make any difference. Just get on with the job of shooting tens. Try to find out for yourself at what speed you achieve the best results: in training try series of shots at different speeds until you are shooting too quickly and making mistakes in technique which will show that you have exceeded your speed. It may well come as a surprise at what speed you obtain the best groups. The style of target changer or system in use will naturally influence your rhythm and must be taken into account. Whereas the three card system may allow a very fast shoot for twenty shots plus sighters, a target box may mean considerably slower technique and a transporter still slower owing to the need to change the target for each shot or wait until the target returns to the firing point. The actual shot release, reloading and sighting may not differ but there will be a pause between each shot. You must become used to all systems so that you are not taken by surprise.

The amount of time taken by the average international shooter is becoming less and less and the shooting times allowed have decreased. This is particularly noticeable with the change from pit marking to electronic targets at 300m. But the shooters themselves are taking less time regardless of the target system: the scores are ever-increasing leading to smaller targets which do not hold people back for long.

9 Training

It has been said that the person who wins the Olympic gold medal is the person who wants it most and if someone else wins it that person wanted it more than you. There is a lot of truth in that, it does not have to be an Olympic gold medal, it can be any first place, from the club championship, league championship, national championship to the world championship. To win consistently you must want to come first; you may even have the attitude that a silver medal means only that you have lost. You do not need to be a good loser, because good losers usually do lose but above all you must be a good competitor. You cannot always come first, and although this may sound very hard it is a competitive world we are in today.

However, you can have a great deal of enjoyment and a lot more fun shooting just to improve your scores, probably even more than the serious dedicated shooter who has to make a very big commitment, but the rewards are equally great. Not monetary rewards in this sport, but receiving the gold medal is far better than any monetary prize. But does the gold medal at the big championship ever feel quite as good as receiving that first badge or award when you started?

Like everybody else the beginner wishes to improve and at the beginner stage this is relatively easy with the learning curve shortened considerably if the help of a competent coach is available. If not, then it is possible at this stage to make rapid improvement by studying leading shooters, photographs of leading shooters and good books on the subject and not just reading them but studying. These should help you to understand what to look for in the shooter or photograph of the shooter, which of course can only show the outer position and not the mental attitude which is all important. It is also necessary to have the will to improve as beyond the beginner stage improving the performance is less easy as fewer dropped points are available to be saved, or a much better way to look at it and a very important one is that there are more tens to be achieved. The shooter, whether beginner or beyond, should not really be interested in the bad shots but how they shot the good shots, however few they may be. It may sound hard to be shooting a string of tens and then have to analyse why you are shooting tens. At first it may be counter-productive but in the long run it is the right way to go about it; it is the correct way to learn – the way of doing things correctly. Anybody can shoot poor shots, so learn how to shoot good ones.

How far you can go in shooting, providing there is nothing much physically wrong, is up to you, but you must have the will to do it, to whatever standard or goal you have set yourself. Set your sights as high as you wish but on the way set intermediate goals which can be achieved with effort. Some shooters will put in maximum effort and set very high standards to be achieved, whilst others will set lower standards but be just as pleased, it depends what you wish to achieve in this sport. You will only get out of it what you are prepared to put in.

Whatever your goal may be for the season or year, plot a curve towards that goal from the standard at which you are starting. That curve will tend to rise fairly rapidly early on and gradually taper off towards the goal as it becomes progressively more difficult. If the results achieved fall short of that curve try to improve the performance both technically

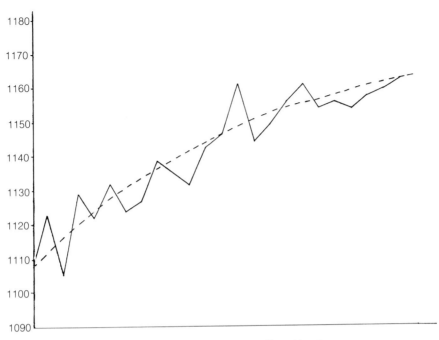

*3 × 40 projections and actual results. First part easily achieved,
later falling behind, and finally once again achieving the goal.*

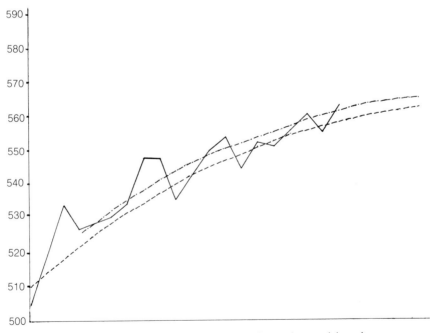

*3 × 20 projections and actual results. Progress better than anticipated, so
projection raised and this more difficult goal was achieved.*

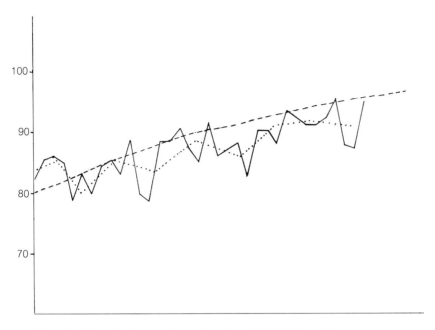

10m air rifle projections and actual results. Individual ten shot scores, plotted and averages for each day (dotted line).

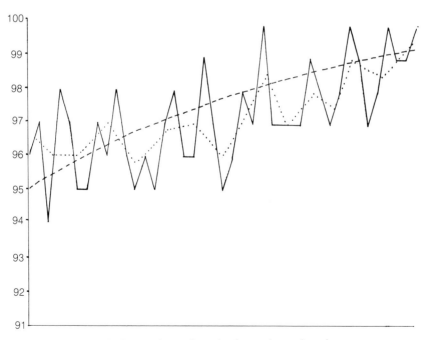

25yds prone projections and actual results for an inexperienced shooter. Individual ten shot scores plotted and averages for each day (dotted line).

and mentally. If, however, the results achieved plot above the line do not tell yourself that you can soft pedal, but instead move that line up to make a higher goal at the end.

These graphs can be just as instructive and fun to the recreational shooter as to the dedicated shooter and it is suggested that one is kept for each position or discipline and each score plotted thereon, together with the average for that day in a different colour. You can therefore additionally see whether the individual scores are becoming more consistent or whether there are highs and lows, as well as seeing the overall improvement.

Think positively: you can shoot tens, you have proved that; you can shoot some more and on the way find out why you are shooting tens. You certainly do not want to know how to shoot poor shots, leave that knowledge to someone else.

THE MENTAL APPROACH

Shooting has been called the sport of the will and although the overall approach has been mentioned already it must be emphasised that correct and positive mental control is needed. An individual must find his or her correct arousal level at which they perform best. Most shooters tend to need to reduce the arousal level at a match but a few find that they have to raise theirs. If the arousal level is too high, the shooter will then feel nervous, call it jitters or whatever. Jitters in most cases is just a different feeling, and this feeling being different to normal worries some people. But if you realise that the heightened arousal level will give you better co-ordination, better sight, better hearing, better touch and smell etc., what is there to worry about? Nothing, only the different feeling, so say to yourself: good, I have that different feeling today, now that I know that it helps me I will do better. And you will, but if your arousal level is not high enough you will feel as if you are not concerned about

the shoot and most likely will come away with a dismal score. If you have a little bit of 'the jitters' you will do much better. It is only harmful when you say to youself, I feel different today, I have the jitters, I do not understand this, and then let yourself be taken on to the next stage when they can harm the performance. Once you understand it you will not be worried but will be pleased and so will do well.

If, however, you do find that your arousal level is too low, the cure is simple; just say to yourself, if I continue like this I will come last, and that will arouse you. One of the best international shooters has this problem on the first few shots, and uses this method as a cure. If you find your arousal level does get too high the best form of mental control is Autogenics, a passive form of mental control which can be learnt over a period of some weeks and then kept in as part of the normal training programme. When you are at those important matches you can use Autogenics to give you the arousal level you have found best for top performance. It should be taught by a qualified person as it can be very powerful but only a few phrases are needed by the shooter. Whereas we should be able to control our bodies directly with out minds and a few can, most shooters use phrases to do the same thing. It is very similar to the jingles everybody remembers to jog their memory, in learning the number of days in the year or such like.

It is necessary if you are to become one of the best shooters to be able to have control over your body and its various muscle groups and control over your mind. Even the recreational shooter who shoots for enjoyment only will get more out of the sport if not frustrated by small things over which he apparently has little control.

DRY TRAINING

Dry training or shooting is conducted without ammunition. It is not always possible to get to the range and even if it is, dry training should be a regular habit. When a live shot is fired some errors may be masked by the wish to achieve scores or look at groups and this may spoil the technique but when dry training there is no such exterior influence to divert the attention. All that is needed is an aiming mark set at the correct height at which to aim. The rifle must of course be treated as if it is loaded and this cannot be too highly stressed. Also, if the rifle does not have a dry firing device, insert an empty case into the chamber to prevent possible damage to the firing pin or the chamber itself. When training in this manner it is possible to see exactly what happens when the firing pin falls both before and during follow through. Errors which could otherwise be masked by recoil or the eagerness to see the result are visible, but more importantly when a perfect dry shot is released the shooter can see why and learn what is being done right. Small changes to equipment or position can be analysed more effectively to see whether the change is an improvement or not. Remember to change only one thing at a time otherwise the good or bad may be masked.

THE TRAINING PROGRAMME

If you are to improve rapidly or achieve the best results of which you are capable you should draw up a training programme. Even if you are a recreational shooter it is still much nicer to make progress and see your scores increase along a step-by-step guide. The step from a recreational shooter to a dedicated shooter is a big step and the majority will not wish to take it even if they have the time and ability. The type of training programme for the dedicated shooter has to be made out for the individual and it is most intensive but still based on the same principles. Each action in the act of shooting is broken down and each part made as perfect as possible then gradually brought

together, with the object that if each part is as perfect as possible then the whole will be as well.

To go as far and/or as fast as possible it is not just a matter of going to the range and shooting with all the attendant factors that have to be brought together at one and the same time. It is necessary to decide what your goal may be and how far ahead you are looking and plan to try your best to achieve it. Your aim may be for example to boost your average in air rifle from 85 to 95 in say nine months, or to have a scoring ability to make your national squad within a similar period. Don't forget to set intermediate goals as well as your long-term goals.

A training programme can be broken down into three headings: the first, a standard of fitness to be achieved that is going to allow you to achieve your main goal; the second, any special exercises that you may need for shooting; and thirdly the technical programme for the increase of your shooting performance. Details of exercises for achieving a general overall standard of fitness are well detailed in many books and should be according to age and sex. If any lifting of weights is to be involved they should not be heavy but go for moderate weights and high repetitions. Special exercises for shooting are for endurance whilst still, and for achieving a good sense of balance. Additionally it is necessary to develop control over the muscles and to learn how to relax them.

To achieve the endurance necessary to hold the rifle without fatigue, the rifle itself or another object of similar weight can be held in position for increasingly longer periods of time. To improve the balance, cycling is very good, as is trying to balance the bicycle whilst stationary. Try other exercises such as balancing on one leg then the other on a beam or narrow piece of wood securely fixed to the floor. There are many variations of exercise capable of improving the balance and, indeed, many of the ballet dancers' routines are ideal for shooting.

Stretching exercises are necessary to ensure that the shooter is flexible, particularly for the standing position and to some degree the other positions; a greater degree of flexibility than the average person possesses is required. They also help to relax the various muscle groups. It must be realised that no amount of exercise will take the place of actual shooting and that it is complementary, but do remember to perform warm-up exercises before shooting – any machinery works better warmed up including the human body.

The technical programme for shooting must break down the whole act of shooting into its parts. Holding the rifle without sighting or aiming or any attempt at trigger control and also getting regularly into position without the heavy shooting coat so that better stability may be built up are two examples. Aiming without trigger control is best done against a white target without any aiming mark; this can be added later. With dry firing on the white target, again the aiming mark may be added later. Mentally fire the shot, holding the rifle, aiming and in the mind going through exactly the firing of the shot without actually doing so. This can be alternated so that some shots are live, some dry whilst others are mental in the same training exercise. Trigger control should also be done without aiming and one method of doing this is to find a dark room without any distracting light and just hold the rifle; you and the rifle will get to know each other more quickly this way and the inner feeling will be developed more rapidly. Any movement will be felt and this can then be repeated with trigger control added and as you cannot see in the dark room, aiming will not distract the mind from the separate actions.

This may seem involved and many recreational shooters may not do any of this but it can achieve rapid results if it is planned carefully and then adhered to. Skills fall off if not trained at whatever standard. Try and shoot at least once a week and even

the dedicated shooter should have one day off each week as well. It does not need to be boring and improved scores soon remove any thoughts of not wishing to continue the programme. Special competitions or games can be built in, such as step shooting, where you start with a certain score for ten shots, then a more difficult score for five, increasing the difficulty for three, then two until finally the one shot has to be very good. This can be adjusted to suit whatever standard you are able to achieve and even the better shooters may find the necessity to shoot the final ten in the standing position, even if they average well, a challenge. It can be performed prone only of course.

It is not intended to give a specific programme here as these could vary greatly; you should seek out your club coach and explain what you are trying to achieve and a plan can be built for your own requirements and time available. A word of caution if you are over thirty and/or have any belief that you may have a physical problem: do consult a doctor first before undertaking any physical exercise.

It is sensible for any shooter to keep a shooting diary and essential for the shooter who wishes to get anywhere. Not only should it contain information as to adjustments used on the rifle and equipment so that these can easily be returned to but also details of training programmes and progress. After each training session the diary should be written up with details of what you have done, what you have achieved and exactly the way you felt both externally and internally during the training session. Finally write down what you feel you have achieved. You do not need to be a writer to keep this diary, just put down how you felt it was in your own words which can be a great help as it will enable you to think a particular thing through and can be referred to later on for guidance.

Success lies, not in achieving what you aim at, but in aiming at what you ought to achieve.

COACHES AND COACHING

There are many instructors but few coaches and the type of coaching required at club level is vastly different from that required in the international scene. Every club should have its club instructors and if it is fortunate it may have coaches too. Most countries have some form of national scheme so that instructors and coaches can become qualified and receive regular updates to keep abreast of new developments and techniques. Some countries are particularly fortunate in that they have highly qualified and very able people and, although many countries are not so fortunate, there is no reason why others should not be able to learn a great deal from what more fortunate countries are doing. A great deal of literature is printed and usually available although it may need translating, but surely that is not too big a chore for the information that then becomes available.

The instructor can show a shooter how to do it whereas a coach can extract the best performance out of that individual, and inspire the shooter to even higher performance. There has to be a good relationship between the coach and the shooter; the coach must have a positive attitude, and not only be in control of the shooter but also in control of himself. He (or she) must be able to compartment his life so that if he is not a full-time coach, time must be divided between coaching, the job and home. Even if the coach is a full-time professional, coaching and the home must be kept separate or else the coach will not be fully effective.

The coach must plan the training programme with the shooter and if the programme is for an international shooter it should be planned with meticulous care in order to achieve the best results. The plans for short and medium term must dovetail together with the overall long-term plan, and by constructing these plans for the shooter the coach can ensure success and guard against failure. The coach must be continually learning and adapting to the developing technology of the sport. He or she must be able to plan well as time cannot be regained. The coach in this sport does not need to have been a brilliant shot but it is better if the coach has had a taste of shooting at the highest level if he aspires to be an international coach, otherwise he cannot really know what the shooter may feel on the firing point, or how to cope with the various situations that may occur.

The coach must know the rules, if not by heart at least know where to look if in any doubt as it is no good advising the shooter only to find that it is contrary to some rule or other. The coach must ensure that he is just as ready for the big match as the shooter he is helping to prepare.

Further Reading

Herrigel, Eugen. *Zen and the Art of Archery.* Routledge and Kegan Paul, first published, 1953

Krilling, William. *Shooting for Gold.* Georgia, USA, 1986

Pullum, B., and Hanenkrat, F. T. *Position Rifle Shooting.* Winchester Press, USA, 1973

Successful Shooting. National Rifle Association, USA, 1981

UIT Journal. Official publication of the UIT, Munich (bi-monthly)

United States Markmanship Unit. *International Rifle Marksmanship Guide.* Georgia, 1983

Yur'yev, A. A. *Competitive Shooting.* National Rifle Association, USA, 1985

Useful Addresses

Secretary General
Union Internationale de Tir
UIT, Bavariaring 21
D – 8000 München 2
West Germany

National Rifle Association
Bisley Camp
Brookwood
Woking
Surrey GU24 0PB
England

The National Small-Bore Rifle Association
Lord Roberts House
Bisley Camp
Brookwood
Woking
Surrey GU24 0NP
England

Australian Shooting Association
PO Box NI48
Grosvenor Street
Sydney 2000
Australia

Shooting Federation of Canada
333 River Road
Vanier City
Ontario K1L 8B9
Canada

National Shooting Federation
  of New Zealand
PO Box 1939
Wellington
New Zealand

National Rifle Association of America
1600 Rhode Island Avenue NW
Washington DC 20036
USA

Index

Italic numerals denote page number of illustrations.